AGILE PROJECT MANAGEMENT

QuickStart Guide

SECOND EDITION

The Simplified Beginner's Guide to Agile Project Management

Second Edition Created December 8, 2016

Editor : Marilyn Burkley

Cover Illustration and Design: Katie Poorman, Copyright © 2016 by ClydeBank Media LLC
Interior Design: Katie Poorman, Copyright © 2016 by ClydeBank Media LLC

ClydeBank Media LLC
P.O Box 6561
Albany, NY 12206
Printed in the United States of America

Copyright © 2016
ClydeBank Media LLC
www.clydebankmedia.com
All Rights Reserved

ISBN : 978-1502393463

contents

Terms displayed in ***bold italic*** can be found
defined in the glossary, starting on page 153.

&

Feel free to take notes beginning on page 156.

introduction

Some activities are only possible to execute successfully if they are associated with more than one person. They are either too extensive in their magnitude or too sophisticated in their nature to be performed by a single individual. They require too much work or a diversity of expertise that no one person possesses. It is then necessary to approach these activities using a team.

In addition to the overarching aim of satisfying the original objective, any project, whether in commerce or broader society, requires proper planning and execution, so that the available resources of time, money, and labor are appropriately utilized. The management of projects in this way is a distinct discipline in the corporate sphere, replete with its various styles and their proponents. Consider, for instance, China's famous Three Gorges Dam. This dam, which was completed in the early 2000s, is a truly gargantuan structure. The dam secures a reservoir 660 km in length containing approximately nine cubic miles of water weighing forty billion tons. This mass of water is so substantial that it actually affects the rotation of the earth to a slight yet significant extent, and it has shifted the position of the magnetic poles by nearly an inch. Its hydroelectric installation generates power equivalent to about twenty nuclear power reactors. The Three Gorges Dam is not only a marvel of engineering, it's also a marvel of project management. Machines and materials must be procured. People have to be employed. Plans have to be drawn out, and everything must be coordinated intelligently.

But what if you could, with a simple stroke of a key, move an entire team of workers (or a crane for that matter) from one side of the

594-foot-wide Three Gorges Dam to the opposite side? What if you could move, resize, and reconfigure the dam's massive turbines at will and perform hundreds of real-world tests measuring the energy output of the dam across a multitude of configurations? Would such flexibility change your approach to project management?

Information technology is more flexible and at times more unpredictable than the physical materials employed at a construction site. If you attempted to pursue an IT project—software development, let's say—the same way you pursue the building of a dam, with an end-to-end ironclad blueprint of your build and a strict production schedule, then your lack of flexibility would likely prohibit you from delivering an optimal product. Your project management approach would be much stronger if you incorporated an element of intelligent flexibility on your path to achieving the best possible result. On the flip side, if you tried to build a dam "flexibly," without the aid of a fairly precise blueprint, then you'd be likely to waste copious amounts of time, money, and resources or, worse, build a dam that could not stand.

From massive public works projects to the creation of complex IT services, the concerns of *project management* persistently come into play. Many considerations of project management are universal, such as budget, design considerations, construction methods, time frame, marketability, key specifications, and performance thresholds. The approaches used when assessing these considerations, however, are not universal and will prove dramatically different depending on the nature of the project. A simple copy and paste can move miles of powerful code; the same agility is not felt in matters of concrete, stone, and lumber. Agile is a popular methodology of modern project management that, while particularly fitting for software development endeavors, can be applied across a broad range of production environments. This book examines Agile in detail, including its history, its techniques, and its implications for those who use it. The book begins by exploring the relevance of project management at large. It then proceeds to work through the various aspects of Agile before reviewing the Envision, Speculate, Explore, Adapt, and Close phases of Agile Project Management. A series of case studies in Agile are reviewed in the later chapters, followed by a review of the popular criticisms that have been directed at Agile. There is also an overview of the Agile sub-industry that has arisen, in terms of both advisory services and the software tools that its use necessitates.

This book is intended as an introduction to the Agile Project Management system.

fig. 1

#	CHAPTER CONTENTS
1	Presents an overview of the concept of project management and illustrates principles that are germane to the entire subject
2	Explains the origins, history, and founding principles of Agile
3	Examines Agile's core structure
4–8	Introduces and explores the basic phases of Agile Project Management (APM) framework
9	Surveys the multiple popular methodologies of APM, including Scrum and Lean
10	Introduces the software tools used to implement Agile
11–14	Discusses practical applications of Agile Project Management illustrated by case studies
15	Discusses possible issues arising from such application
16	Looks at the key industry players in Agile training and consulting, along with a list for further reading

Those interested in applying Agile to their projects, either as an experiment or on the basis of a more serious recommendation, should remember that the information provided by this text is general in nature and does not constitute specific professional advice or organizational strategy. As a preliminary source of information, however, it should enable the reader to pursue deeper inquiries and ultimately decide on the suitability of the Agile system and, once that has been established, the exact variation to apply.

Finally, though our contemporaries may not all be in agreement, this text will treat "Agile" as a proper noun while concurrently acknowledging that Agile methodologies span many industries and encompass several distinctly defined frameworks. Nevertheless, we take the position that "Agile Project Management" (APM), can signify a distinct structure (Envision, Speculate, Explore, Adapt, Close), per the outline presented in Chapters 3 through 7.

| 1 |
History of Agile Project Management

The Agile Alliance

The concept of a standardized or prescribed strategy for project management is not new. Different organizations or cultures may have practiced their own methods in regulating large labor forces or assigning resources to the projects in which they engaged. However, it was only since the middle of the 1950s that the concept began to be regarded as a more formal discipline and attract its official terminology. At present, it is taken seriously in commerce and elsewhere, as evidenced by, for example, the Association for Project Management (APM) in the UK or the American Society for the Advancement of Project Management (ASAPM).

Agile Project Management to large extent represents a reformation of or departure from several of the preexisting 20th century project management methodologies. Therefore, the formulation and subsequent promotion of a discrete and self-contained management methodology is not a novelty, nor is it surprising that it draws on existing systems of both project and business management.

Agile Project Management (or Agile for short) was devised within the software industry. The process of creating new software is known specifically as "development." The initiators of the Agile doctrine were all software developers. This is possibly why it has such a strong association with the IT sector. Proponents of Agile have made the assertion that it is applicable to any industry, and there is literature examining how this has happened in practice. Its potential for deployment in activities outside of IT will be discussed in later chapters of this book.

In early 2000, correspondence about project management techniques was started between the eventual Agile role players. This initial interest blossomed into a formal conference in Chicago in 2001.[1] There, seventeen professionals in the software industry hashed out a new method, based on their experience with their respective, preferred alternatives. At this meeting, they composed the various statements that have become synonymous with the Agile movement.

First, they identified what are regarded as the three erroneous assumptions in project management:

1. It is possible to plan a large project.
   (Meaning that it's possible to more or less anticipate and map out the development and result of a project from beginning to end with a high degree of clarity and predictability)

2. It is possible to protect against late changes.
   (Meaning that late changes are not inevitable)

3. It makes sense to lock in big projects early.
   (Meaning that resources on a large scale should be acquired early and in full, because there is no chance of any wavering from stated plans)

As you can see, these three issues all highlight the point raised at the end of the previous chapter: that the objective of a project (or the

---

[1] Jim Highsmith, "History: The Agile Manifesto," *AgileManifesto.org*, 2001, http://agilemanifesto.org/history.html.

end user's expectations) can change during the course of its execution and make it impossible for the project team to provide a satisfactory result. The first assumption on the list is an allusion to the immensity of some projects and how they are not amenable to a rigid and detailed framework or forecasting. Even a simple job like painting a house depends on stable weather. How much more so, then, the construction of a dam spanning an entire mountain range, or a software application attempting to compete in a space where new competitors enter the market on a daily basis?

The meeting proceeded to identify four binary juxtapositions, showing preference for a new approach to project management.

fig. 2

Individuals & Interactions *over* Processes & Tools
Working Software *over* Comprehensive Documentation
Customer Collaboration *over* Contract Negotiation
Responding to Change *over* Following a Plan

The idea is that while there is value in the items on the right-hand side, the items on the left-hand side should be valued more.

The last item is particularly noteworthy here, but the others also serve to illustrate the emphasis on people instead of procedure (the first item), on the efficacy of the end result rather than the bureaucratic administration of its development and presence in the market (the second item), and on customer service and satisfaction over impersonal, disinterested business practice (item three).

It should be stated that the emphasis on reducing the administration associated with a project (its bureaucracy or "comprehensive documentation") sometimes attracts the adjective "lightweight" in the context of Agile (as opposed to the "heavyweight" systems that encompass extensive administration and management structures).

In trying to establish these principles as the elements of a project management strategy in practice, the meeting resulted in the creation of the 12 Principles of Agile Software (figure 3).

This list of principles is known in the industry as the Agile Manifesto, and it has been officially published on the website of the Agile Alliance, which consists of the original seventeen members who drafted it:

- Kent Beck
- Mike Beedle
- Arie van Bennekum
- Alistair Cockburn
- Ward Cunningham
- Martin Fowler
- James Grenning
- Jim Highsmith
- Andrew Hunt
- Ron Jeffries
- Jon Kern
- Brian Marick
- Robert C. Martin
- Steve Mellor
- Ken Schwaber
- Jeff Sutherland
- Dave Thomas

fig. 3

1 Our highest priority is to satisfy the customer through early and continuous delivery of valuable software.

2 Welcome changing requirements, even late in development. Agile processes harness change for the customer's competitive advantage.

3 Deliver working software frequently, from a couple of weeks to a couple of months, with a preference to the shorter timescale.

4 Business people and developers must work together daily throughout the project.

5 Build projects around motivated individuals. Give them the environment and support they need, and trust them to get the job done.

6 The most efficient and effective method of conveying information to and within a development team is face-to-face conversation.

7 Working software is the primary measure of progress.

8 Agile processes promote sustainable development. The sponsors, developers, and users should be able to maintain a constant pace indefinitely.

9 Continuous attention to technical excellence and good design enhances agility.

10 Simplicity, the art of maximizing the amount of work not done, is essential.

11 The best architectures, requirements, and designs emerge from self-organizing teams.

12 At regular intervals, the team reflects on how to become more effective, then tunes and adjusts its behavior accordingly.
(http://www.agilemanifesto.org)

There is no need to enter into a detailed analysis of these individuals or their careers in the IT industry. What is important to note is that some of them represented the most prominent existing management paradigms at the time. These were Extreme Programming (Kent Beck), Adaptive Software Development (Jim Highsmith), Feature-Driven Development, Pragmatic Programming (Andrew Hunt and Dave Thomas), Crystal (Alistair Cockburn), Scrum (Ken Schwaber and Jeff Sutherland), and Dynamic Systems Development Method (DSDM). Some of these paradigms are either closely associated with Agile or are regarded as its subsidiary methodologies. What is also obvious from the members' names is that they are related to software development.

One contributor who does merit individual mention is Jim Highsmith, who has gone on to create a reputation for himself as the leading authority on the Agile Project Management methodology. We will be referring to the published work of Highsmith at various points throughout this text.

Motivation

The desire to establish a new, more effective, or otherwise improved project management system in the software industry was based on advertised and substantial dissatisfaction with existing methods. This was perhaps due to the expansion of the IT industry, in terms of both scale and range of application, or merely because the nature of its product makes it the territory for this type of experimentation.

By the year 2000, the Internet, software, and computer technology were the machinery of the future; even smaller, local industries were irrevocably tech-dependent. The tech genie had said farewell to its bottle a long time ago, and the relevance of the Internet and IT would be an inevitable hallmark of the twenty-first century. People may not remember the Y2K crisis (the phenomenon that arose as a result of the inability of some software to process more than two digits for the year in a date, rendering it useless on January 1, 2000) or how excited economists and other commercial observers became with the introduction of IT into each new sphere of economic activity. But the overarching sentiment of the time was one of expectation, complete with all the sci-fi style imaginative prediction that goes with it.

With the IT industry being required to supply solutions on such a massive scale to so many different markets, a refined or even entirely new management approach was a priority, especially one which is so uniquely suited to the industry itself. As an example, Windows 95, an earlier Microsoft operating system (which some younger readers may have to Google to identify), sold 40 million copies in its first year. Microsoft's latest offering, Windows 10, reached 75 million users in four weeks.[2]

One fundamental characteristic of software and its development that may make it susceptible to trouble is what the industry terms "uncertainty." This is more in connection with the already outlined unstable nature of a project and its targeted results. The development of new software is uncertain in that its ultimate desired functionality cannot be determined until it is in use by the customer.

Sometimes the end user's expectations change once the software is in use, since they may realize new possibilities or receive more decisive feedback from their own target market. Because of this, the software developer is tasked with creating a product that is satisfactory but that simultaneously has to subscribe to the potentially shifting requirements of its commissioner. This is known as "scope creep," and the opportunity it presents for failure, frustration, and miscommunication is obvious.

Prior to the formalized advent of Agile, management protocols revolved around two basic approaches, the latter of which would evolve into what we recognize today as "Agile":

---

[2] Jared Newman, "Four weeks after launch, Windows 10 is already on 75 million PCs and tablets," *PCWorld*, August 26, 2016, http://www.pcworld.com/article/2975911/windows/four-weeks-after-launch-windows-10-is-already-on-75-million-pcs-and-tablets.html.

Waterfall

Waterfall is the protocol most popularly mentioned in conjunction with Agile and is often seen as an opposing or antiquated methodology. It involves developing the software according to a prior plan or determined framework of activity, like the stages in the rapids of a waterfall. It is sometimes referred to as "plan-driven."

Spiral, rapid prototyping, evolutionary delivery & incremental delivery

All of these approaches entail the production of pieces of the ultimate product, for the customer to experiment with and provide a response to. They are sometimes described as "agile," that is, as opposed to the execution of a premeditated plan.

The incremental or phased nature of the second approach proved more compatible with the development of software, modulating the uncertainty that's often innate to the development process. Understanding Agile as a departure from Waterfall is critical and will be revisited several times throughout this text. In assessing the various sub-methodologies that have arisen under the Agile umbrella, it is important to remember what preceded it (Waterfall) and how successive innovations and spin-off methodologies contributed to our present notion of "Agile."

Chapter Recap

- Agile was born of the software industry's need for innovative approaches to project management.

- Agile offers a solution for unique uncertainties that affect the IT industry's ability to develop products.

- The Waterfall (pre-Agile) method of project management offers a useful comparison point when studying Agile Project Management.

| 2 |
Basic Strategy

In This Chapter
- Distinctions Between Agile & Waterfall
- Comparative 5-Step Processes That Define Agile & Waterfall
- Agile's Application of Flexibility as a Response to Unpredictability

Agile (adj.): Able to move quickly and easily

General Outline

Agile Project Management, as the name suggests, is a rapid and highly responsive method of process management. Its leading proponent, Jim Highsmith, has written that it enables a much faster, more flexible response to changing market circumstances and the sudden, unexpected tactics of competitors.[3] That is, essentially, how it has come to have the adjective as its official name—due to the supposedly malleable and reflexive nature of the processes to which it is applied.

For this propensity, Agile relies on the phased or staged process structure that it represents. Instead of the more traditional Waterfall approach, whereby the project is defined, its parameters stated, and then its constituent steps taken, Agile allows for self-terminating phases or increments. At the end of each phase, or "iteration," the customer is presented with a usable product and their feedback is sought in order to modify the next increment. This incremental or iterative approach eventually arrives at the final product or ultimate result.

---

[3] Highsmith, *AgileManifesto.org.*

It should be apparent from this description that Agile makes an adapted end result possible. During the project, the customer or end user can assist in determining its course, by supplying additional information or changing their expectations entirely.

During the early twentieth century, millions of immigrants came to the United States in search of a better life. They often had very little money to spend, and so adopted a method of home building that many in the modern day might find perplexing. Once they had saved enough money to buy a plot of land, they would construct only the basement on the land. The basement would be their residence until they had accumulated enough money to add one or two stories. Such a development approach is similar to the Agile system insofar as the customer (homeowner) is presented with a finished and workable stage of the product at the end of each iteration. If their funds are exhausted or if they realize that they no longer require further development, they can terminate the process entirely.

In other ways, the home building analogy is much more similar to the traditional Waterfall method of project management. The materials used in constructing a home can't be rapidly moved, copied, or deleted from the build like a line of code. Moreover, the functions served by a home are fairly apparent out of the gate, whereas the development of software may be driven and diverted by real-time feedback from customers and fast-paced advances in technological capacity; new processors come to market a lot faster than new building materials. The iPhone's "iOS" operating system has gone through countless iterations since the iPhone's 2007 debut, each iOS update seemingly capable of evolving the product from the inside out as opposed to merely supplying add-on features. This nuanced, non-linear, and fast-paced character of software development is one of the reasons that the need for alternatives to traditional project management methods became apparent. Agile was born out of this need.

Basic Strategy

The most important steps in the project management system prescribed by Agile are adapted from a more traditional paradigm. Previously, project management terminology included five steps in the process. Highsmith invented his own five steps as analogous to those and in accordance with the underlying philosophy of his own system.

fig. 4

Waterfall	Agile
Initiating	Envisioning
Planning	Speculating
Executing	Exploring
Controlling	Adapting
Closing	Closing

The Initiating and Planning stages in the traditional Waterfall process involve identifying what the customer wants and then planning how to provide it, which happens during the Executing stage. Agile, on the other hand, uses the looser terms of Envisioning and Speculating to describe the first two stages, and then Exploring to refer to the actual implementation of the plan. This is because in Agile, the execution of that specific increment does not represent the sole or entire execution phase of the project and, generally, the project is not subject to a fixed product description. Customer feedback is sought and applied to the next phase, Exploring. This, in turn, means that the product is "adapted" rather than "controlled."

The use of language in these five steps is indicative of the Agile approach. The rigid, narrow philosophy behind the traditional management system is replaced by the more flexible, responsive attitude of Agile. In Chapter 3, we'll take a more expansive, in-depth look at each of these five steps.

In assessing Agile, it is important to remember that the system was devised in order to improve the development of new products. Highsmith describes the following five main imperatives for Agile's application:

fig. 5

CONTINUOUS INNOVATION
└→ Staying current with the customer's needs

PRODUCT ADAPTABILITY
Anticipating the customer's future needs ←┘

REDUCED DELIVERY SCHEDULES
└→ Matching supply with changing market demand

ADAPTABILITY
People and processes match market pace ←┘

RELIABLE RESULTS
└→ Reduce variation and improve forecasting

Agile is referred to as iterative because it involves an itinerant (phased) process with which to fulfill the customer's needs. It is incremental because it does so in stages of completion. The priority is to produce something at the end of each stage that the customer can use, that fits a clear business need. These stages of completion are commonly referred to as *sprints*. Sprints are the essential development unit (building block) in Agile Project Management. They are typically one week to one month in duration. They are team-based bursts of work that focus on the development of a specific, agreed-upon set of "features" (see chapter 3). The Agile Project Management's sprint-based approach, as opposed to that of Waterfall, often proves a better fit for businesses that must navigate constantly changing landscapes to remain competitive. It is also useful for businesses that want to produce products fast that can accommodate immediate business needs.

Scope & Staff

In keeping with its emphasis on an unknown or unpredictable project outcome, Agile does not specify the final product, as the plan-driven (Waterfall) methods do. In the latter, the product or outcome (the scope) of the project is the first item of interest. Estimates are then made as to the entire cost and time frame of the project. Often, budgets are overrun and additional time is required.

Agile, however, does not specify an exact scope (as is seen in the strikingly inexact terms used to describe its initial steps—Envisioning, Speculating, and even Exploring to refer to its execution). Rather, its focus is on the available resources of time and money. In this way, the project cannot exceed those parameters. Also, as an iterative process, it allows the customer to terminate their involvement at the end of any iteration, leaving them with a usable product, even if it is not the entire or ultimate output that they initially desired. It is, therefore, theoretically impossible for an Agile project to surpass the available capital investment or its deadline.

This approach also has implications for how staff participation in the project is managed. Agile does not tolerate the more traditional top-down (vertical) power dynamic in the management of the project team. Instead, the team members are encouraged to take ownership of the project and manage themselves to a large extent. Certain team leaders are used in Agile merely to negotiate or remove institutional obstructions and maintain an environment that is conducive to the team's work and success. It is the team itself that sets the work agenda and decides on the proper approach.

All of these factors will become more apparent in Chapters 3 through 8, as we explore the component parts of the Agile Project Management Life Cycle (or "Framework") in depth, and in Chapter 8, as we discuss various Agile-specific methodologies.

Chapter Recap

- The components of Agile Project Management correlate with the traditional Waterfall method but offer greater flexibility.

- Agile uses an incremental approach to completing projects based on work units called "sprints."

- Team dynamics in an Agile working environment are not as hierarchical as they are in traditional working environments.

| 3 |

The Envision Phase

The five steps—Envision, Speculate, Explore, Adapt, Close—as introduced in the previous chapter are referred to as the *Agile Project Management Framework* or, sometimes, as the Agile Project Management Life Cycle. The names of the five steps themselves were first recorded by Jim Highsmith, seemingly in response to the key tenets of the Waterfall method. Everything about the APM Framework, especially when compared to Waterfall, is an endorsement of flexibility. The Waterfall term "planning," for instance, was rejected in favor of "speculating," because planning carries with it the connotation of a fixed road map, where the core parameters (the roads themselves) aren't expected to change. "Speculating," by contrast, allows for more unexpected events, shifts, perhaps changes in available resources or changes in the demands and expectations of the customers, or even changes in the goals of the project management team itself. "Explore" (the third step) is really the execution phase, but because explore is a less rigid term than "execute," the team can operate with greater flexibility and agility. Because they're exploring, there's less risk of

29

being overcautious, too afraid of making a mistake, too reluctant to attempt creative solutions. If you're "exploring" then you're still gathering answers, even as you're asserting them, and this disposition, Agile finds, makes for optimal project management.

Figure 6 shows how the life cycle phases proceed throughout the course of a project. You'll notice that the Speculate, Explore, and Adapt phases are iterative and may recur several times throughout the life of a project. The Envision and Close phases, by contrast, are one-time only.

fig. 6

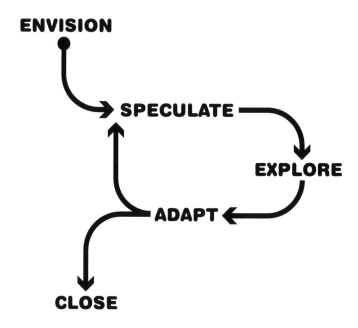

Highsmith makes the argument that the static Waterfall-style methods are useful if the business is pursuing "repeatable manufacturing," but if the business is pursuing "reliable innovation," then Agile Project Management is more likely to yield optimal results. By following the steps in the Agile Project Management Framework, the ongoing, meaningful, and valuable education of team members becomes possible, if not inevitable. And not only does management enjoy a high level of visibility into the project management process as it unfolds, but others in the organization—teams, managers, and any other interested parties—are able to inspect and learn from the process being followed by any given team.

As companies, organizations, or even teams grow larger, it becomes more and more difficult to pursue meaningful, enduring changes to established processes. Consistent reliance on the Agile Project Management Framework allows teams to be ever more flexible, even as they grow.

Creating a vision for a new product, service, or process improvement should occur before any strategic approach is considered. By the time you're developing strategy (mainly in the Speculate phase) you're already considering the "how" of the project, when you first need to consider the "what." Author, publisher, and "visionary" Michael Hyatt argues that our visions, when cultivated, have a way of attracting the strategy needed to bring them to life. On his blog, Your Virtual Mentor, Hyatt recounts a personal story where the strength of his vision was able to turn around a failing enterprise. His supervisor had resigned unexpectedly, and Hyatt was made head of his division. The division was failing, the least profitable out of seven in the company. Rather than "being reasonable" and keeping expectations low for his division, Hyatt decided to go on a retreat for several days with the intent of developing a bold and optimistic vision for success. He created a simple plan containing targets for various performance metrics. Upon returning, Hyatt called a meeting with his staff. Although he was frank with them about the current condition of the division and the challenges ahead, he presented a compelling, specific vision for what he wanted to see them accomplish as a team. Most among Hyatt's staff rolled up their sleeves and committed to bringing the new vision to reality. After a while, even the stragglers and cynics began to believe that a new day was possible. Eighteen months later, and for several years thereafter, Hyatt's division was one of the company's strongest and consistently turned a sizable profit.[4]

In the Envision phase of Agile Project Management, the vision you create should be specific with regard to "what" and "who." A "what" might be something like, "I want to create an augmented reality (AR) video game that will be played by theme park goers on their mobile phones. The game will feature characters that are licensed to be used by the theme park. The characters will provide the game players clues to the locations of various AR artifacts that can be found at certain locations within the theme park. If a player collects a certain number of artifacts, then he can redeem them for prizes at gift shops. This AR game will be downloadable for a one-time fee of $2.99 and will bring in $250,000 in revenue to the park during the first year."

The Project Charter

A *project charter* is used to document the essential vision for a project. The charter is used to define what the project is, who it involves, and what constitutes success. There may be certain abstract and theoretical elements to the charter as well, such as "project mission." In the case of our augmented reality game, the mission would be something to the effect of, "To engage theme park customers in a new and memorable way, while leveraging our intellectual property assets to build profit."

A team may choose to forgo a project charter—for instance, if the project is too small and time is a factor. The decisions about whether to create a charter, how long it should be, and what it should contain must be decisions that your entire team participates in making.

Your project charter can be used to establish and codify priorities. If you're developing an AR game that encourages people to explore

---

[4] Michael Hyatt, "Why Vision Is More Important Than Strategy," *Your Virtual Mentor* (blog), *MichaelHyatt.com*, January 23, 2012, https://michaelhyatt.com/why-vision-is-more-important-than-strategy.html.

a theme park, then you'll want to prioritize safety during the course of product development. Priorities may also be established to define project responsibilities and order of work. For instance, you may want certain employees or contractors involved with the project to always work on programming tasks when possible and to only work on testing tasks if no programming tasks are available. For other employees or contractors you may want to assign exactly the opposite priorities—testing and then programming. Again, defining priorities wherever possible will prevent needless deliberation and expedite production.

In Chapter 3, we discussed how the scopes for projects are defined in Agile Project Management. To summarize, though Agile provides an added level of flexibility, organizations must still be aware of the limits to available time and resources. When scoping a project through Agile Project Management, you should focus first on the overall vision for the project, which will be defined succinctly in the project mission. Don't make the mistake of focusing on the resources you currently have on hand, but instead focus on your vision for the project and what you'd like the project to be, and define your scope accordingly. It's okay to set an ambitious goal. If there simply aren't sufficient resources available to support what you have in mind, then you'll rub up against that reality soon enough. What's most important is that you don't limit yourself too severely right out of the gate. Instead, allow your defined scope to zero in on the nature of your customer. Are we targeting kids, adults, men, women, etc.? What is the essential value we'll be bringing to our customers? Is it entertainment? Is it convenience? Is it improved health? And don't forget to reflect on the "why" of your project, as you define scope. If you don't want your project to go off track, then it's important to maintain and adhere to a clearly defined purpose; in this case, "We're creating an AR game for our theme park to attract visitors to the park and to boost revenue." Record these scoping parameters in your project charter.

Your project charter should detail the various roles and responsibilities of key team members, such as the *project manager* and the *project sponsor*. If the project manager is the CEO of the project, then the project sponsor is like the chairman of the board of directors. There will usually be less hands-on involvement from the project sponsor, but he'll ultimately be responsible for making sure that the project is supplied with money, resources, and workers. He'll be the liaison between the project and executive management, ensuring that they're aware of and support the project. The project manager will be much more concerned with the day-to-day of project operations. When questions on project scope, responsibilities, or priorities arise, the project manager will be the final arbiter. Within a larger organization, the project manager is also responsible for preparing reports that demonstrate the progress of the project and any need for additional resources. The project manager is responsible for keeping the project on track, adhering to the vision, by ensuring that the project is directly servicing the organization's business needs.

A good project charter will also include clear definitions for project success, whether they're revenue targets, customer engagement metrics, ticket sales, efficiency improvements, or the development of a new product that stands out from the competition.

Choosing Tools

Another key component of the Envision phase is the selection and use of effective collaboration tools. The nature of the collaboration tools you choose is largely dependent on the type of project you're managing. If you're working on a large construction site, then two-way radios may be optimal, but if you're working on building an app and your team members are all over the globe, then you'll likely be better off with cloud collaboration tools such as Slack, Quickbase, or Asana. Since Agile Project Management was born in the tech sector, you're likely to find more Agile teams using online collaboration tools, even teams that don't work remotely. Here are some guidelines for the selection and maintenance of *online collaboration tools* for your team.

1. **Be aware of the transition burden.** Veer on the side of using products with which your team members are already familiar. If you feel that the project you're about to embark on warrants a switch, then be aware that you're going to have to onboard (set up) and train team members. That said, many online collaboration tools are very intuitive and your team should be able to learn the software quickly.

2. **Compare collaboration tools while keeping your vision in mind.** Author, blogger, and project management expert Elizabeth Harrin urges project managers not to ignore their gut when choosing project management collaboration tools.[5] You're not going to want to take the time to inspect the programming code of each utility, so at some point you're going to have to use your intuition to determine which tools seem likely to aid your team in reaching its stated objectives.

3. **Be aware of how your team communicates, and choose your collaboration tools appropriately.** One of the major differences, for instance, between Slack and Asana is that Slack makes it easy to jump straight from a chat log to a phone call. If you are in need of an online collaboration tool but some of your team members are more comfortable communicating via voice, then available mediums for voice, text, chat, etc., must be considered. Other considerations along these lines include

---

[5] Elizabeth Harrin, *Collaboration Tools for Project Managers*, (Philadelphia, Project Management Institute, 2016).

the availability of conference calling, screen sharing, and private communications.

4. **Stop using one or more tools when redundancies arise.** You may notice that some of the tools used by your team accomplish essentially the same function; however, you're reluctant to consolidate because you fear there may be some unique information on one or another platform that's not replicated elsewhere. Rather than keeping multiple redundant collaboration tools in place, consider, for example, having your employees download their chat logs, files, or whatever else may be stored in a now obsolete system, into a searchable batch file.

5. **Make sure that at least one of your utilities provides a viewable schedule.** These days, workers expect to have their project work schedule accessible, just as students expect to have access to the course syllabus. People want to know where they are on the roadmap to completion and what comes next. Given that Agile Project Management involves combining a multitude of smaller accomplishments (sprints) into one large accomplishment (the project), you can expect that your team members will want to know where they stand, pretty much at all times. If you do not choose a collaboration utility that offers a shareable, updateable schedule, then be sure that one is accessible elsewhere within the work environment.

Establishing a Healthy Agile Work Culture

The Envision stage must also provide a set of principles for how your Agile team will work together, the norms and decorum to be observed. Agile teams typically work better when they are kept smaller, generally no more than fifteen people. There's no hard rule saying teams can't be larger, but the more team members, the more difficulties may be encountered when cultivating group focus and a careful observation of the envisioned culture. Amazon CEO Jeff Bezos is known for his "two pizza rule," which advises never having a meeting where two pizzas are insufficient to feed the entire group.[6] A smaller team will operate much like a family, just more professionally. There should be an emphasis on focus, respect, and active listening.

In chapter 3 we introduced the concept of "sprints" as the building blocks of production in Agile. Sprints limit the focus of any given component of the project. Team members should be concerned only with the objectives of the current sprint. This can be a difficult task, seeing as it's often tempting to speculate on and criticize the project at large. If a culture is established that limits focus to the current sprint, then it will be easier for the team to come together and work as one toward a clear, immediate objective.

Agile teams tend to emphasize a culture of face-to-face communication over email and text. Emails should not be relied upon for facilitating conversations, especially those that may be contentious. Remote teams may encounter particularly difficult team-building challenges. Tools such as regular meetings, conference calls, and recreational discussion threads can be helpful in making remote teams more comfortable working together.

Another often challenging cultural element that's especially important to a good Agile team is a willingness to respond positively to requests for change. Let's say we're in the middle of developing our AR theme park game—perhaps we're pursuing a sprint where we're mapping out the park using a GPS utility from Google. Our project sponsor comes in to work one day and reports that new safety

---

[6] Vivian Giang, "The 'Two Pizza Rule' Is Jeff Bezos' Secret to Productive Meetings," *Business Insider*, October, 29, 2013, http://www.businessinsider.com/jeff-bezos-two-pizza-rule-for-productive-meetings-2013-10.

regulations for AR gaming have been passed by the state legislature and we're required to use a different, more precise mapping utility for the game. The change will require going back through pages and pages of code, updating APIs (Application Program Interfaces), a whole lot of tedious work. If a healthy Agile culture is present in the team, then they will respond with an optimistic, can-do attitude, and will perhaps use the unanticipated monkey wrench as a chance to review and sharpen up other aspects of the code that could be improved.

Using a Product Data Sheet

The *product data sheet* (PDS) is similar to the project charter, but more concise and metrics-focused. This document will contain the mission statement from the project charter, along with a proposed timeline, an estimate of cost, and a listing of constraints. It may also include information about project priorities that will govern development of the product.

As you may have noted, much of the information on the product data sheet also appears on the project charter. The major differences are 1) the brevity and data-heaviness of the PDS will make it quicker and easier to reference when searching for project specs, and 2) the PDS doesn't pay nearly as much attention to the composition and the functioning of the team; it is instead tightly framed around what the product will ultimately become.

The PDS will contain more highly detailed data than the project charter. When it's being created, it's important for both project workers and stakeholders to have a seat at the table, as the details present in this document will prove relevant to all parties. Stakeholders may include executive level management, the project sponsor, or the end customer. For example, in the case of our amusement park AR gaming example, it's unlikely that the amusement park company has a team of game developers standing by. They will very likely hire another company, a contractor, to build the game for them. When this contractor creates the PDS for the game, the appropriate personnel from the amusement park company should be present and participatory, since they are the customers in this case.

It may be tempting in some situations to hit the ground running rather than worrying about a PDS, or even a project charter. Just keep in mind that a good planning process—and a smartly drawn PDS—has a high likelihood of saving time down the road, not to mention money.

Sprint Planning

Although your sprints don't begin until the Explore phase, it's in the Envision and Speculate phases that you must consider and plan for their duration. In order to do this you must be aware of all deadlines for the project and all features to be included in the project. This information should be readily available to all team members via the PDS. In order to effectively plan your sprint, you must become familiar with a key term in Agile: the "feature." A *feature* is a particular service or functionality that a system provides and that is valued by a client. Features must have both an action and a result component. Examples of features might include the following:

- Reporting error messages to web-form users who fail to fill out a critical field

- Establishing an automated security protocol for a system whereby users are prompted to change their passwords every six weeks

- Reporting the number of students enrolled in a class

For our AR theme park game, a feature might be the creation of an online shopping site that allows players to purchase merchandise featuring characters from the game. Another example of a feature would be the institution of in-game "experience points," an accumulation of data that's scaled to ensure that the users are rewarded for the time they spend playing the game (in our example, they are rewarded with credits they can spend to buy merchandise at the theme park gift shop or perhaps in the online store).

Features come in varying shapes and sizes, and when you're defining the length required for a sprint you must accommodate the anticipated workload required for the features that will be developed during the sprint. You're not likely to know exactly how much work will be required for each feature, but if you're working with an experienced team, then they should be able to offer sound estimates.

fig. 7

FEATURES

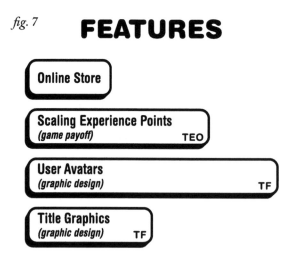

In figure 7 we've quantified our anticipated workloads for various features that will go into the creation of our theme park AR game. If we were to organize these features into two sprints of approximately the same duration, then we'd probably combine the "online store" feature with the "user avatar" feature, and we'd combine the "scaling experience points" feature with the "title graphics" feature. The "scaling experience points" feature will likely require a lot of user testing (therefore it's very time-intensive) and will likely be completed toward the tail end of the project. The graphic design projects (user avatars and title graphics) are a lot more flexible. They can be completed first thing or at the very end. We could test the game with a single avatar (depending on our schedule and priorities, we may even decide to release the game with a single avatar). When planning sprints, it's helpful to tag features that are time flexible with a "tf" in your feature listing, or "teo" for tail end only; see figure 7.

If you're having a lot of trouble determining exactly how much time you'll need for various features, then you can organize your features into broad categories that estimate duration, such as small (20 hours), medium (40 hours), and large (60 hours).

fig. 8

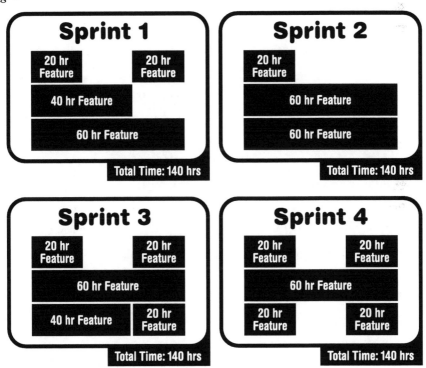

You'll notice in figure 8 that although the features are of varying lengths, the cumulative total time allotment is equal in each sprint

(140 hours). Keeping the duration of sprints uniform is an essential Agile principle, as it allows your team to establish a production rhythm. After your team has completed one sprint, they will begin to develop a strong internal sense of the time they have available to work and they will steadily calibrate their work to fit within the expected time frame. By contrast, if there is a large degree of variety in the time it takes to complete each sprint, a rhythm is hard to establish and the result is waste.

When planning your sprints, the process of determining which features should be developed in which sprints is known as setting up the *sprint structure*. While determining your sprint structure, it's important to make note of which personnel will be available and when. If we hire a video game development company to make an AR game for our amusement park, we may discover that their graphic designers are available only during the fall quarter and have commitments at every other time throughout the year. We can plan our sprint schedule around their availability, ask them to modify their commitments to their other employers, or we can attempt to bring graphic design support to the project either from our own staff or from a third party.

Similar to the task of ensuring the availability of proper personnel is ensuring the availability of general resources, servers, hardware, mobile devices, software, etc. Depending on the size of your organization, there may be other projects under development that are competing for a limited supply of resources.

Business priority is also an important determining factor in defining a sprint structure appropriate for your project. Remember, in theory, each sprint should culminate in some form of usable product; for instance, if we create an online store for our amusement park AR game, then this store should be readily usable elsewhere in the organization. Perhaps the whole store, or at least certain products from it, can be listed elsewhere on other company websites. Always look for opportunities to syndicate the value gained from each feature established. And since certain features are sure to offer more widespread value throughout the business, it only makes sense that business priority will play a role in determining the ordering of your sprint structure.

If you're working with a team that's new to Agile Project Management, then you should include a careful consideration of "risk" when determining which features to put in the early sprints. Risk, in this case, refers to the complexity of the feature being developed. Does the feature require the use of highly sophisticated technology or the cumbersome and error-prone integration of existing code from a previous project into a new build? Is the feature something that's not been attempted before by the organization or requires extensive reliance on interdepartmental communications? Are there too many unknowns involved that could potentially derail feature development? These are all risk factors and should be considered when determining which features to attempt first in the event that the team is new to Agile. If possible, begin with sprints that are simpler in nature; this will imbue the team with confidence and sound rhythm. If newcomers to Agile experience a high level of frustration, then they may be prone to quickly dismissing or giving up on Agile before it's had a real chance to work.

For teams that are rife with experience in Agile, beginning with higher risk sprints is usually the best approach. Experienced Agile teams can use challenging sprints early on in the project to gage and modify important structural issues so as to make the rest of the project run more smoothly.

Though the Speculate phase is invaluable for taking inventory of available resources and stated objectives and for cultivating a vision of success, you won't get too deep into the rigors of sprint planning until your first iteration of the Speculate phase, which we'll discuss in the following chapter.

Chapter Recap

- The Agile Project Management Framework's first phase, Envision, requires teams to create a detailed vision of their completed project.

- Visions should include numerical targets: downloads, dollars, customers, etc.

- The vision for a project should be based on ideal objectives rather than immediate material capabilities.

- The project charter is used to define the mission and success standards for a project.

- Careful selection of collaboration tools will enhance the team's ability to communicate and remain clear on the vision for the project.

- Establishing thoughtful team norms will improve morale by creating a more comfortable work environment.

- The product data sheet offers a summary of data relevant to project progress and objectives.

- Sprints are planned by estimating workloads associated with various features and balancing them out between sprints.

| 4 |

The Speculate Phase

In This Chapter
- Details of Agile's Speculate Phase
- Selecting Features for Sprints
- Feature Requirements
- Product Roadmaps
- How to Organize Feature Production
- User Stories
- Calculating Sprint Velocity

In the previous chapter, we discussed the Envision phase of Agile Project Management, which is a stand-alone phase that's pursued only once per project, at the very beginning. The next phase, the Speculate phase, is one of three phases that iterate multiple times in the life cycle. These iterative phases, Speculate, Explore, and Adapt, are all in play during the course of any given sprint.

The Speculate phase is devoted to determining which features should be released for the immediate iteration (Speculate, Explore, or Adapt). It's also in the Speculate phase that milestones are established aimed at conforming the work done in the iteration to the vision developed during the

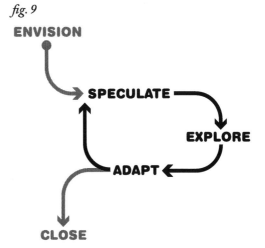

fig. 9

ENVISION

SPECULATE

EXPLORE

ADAPT

CLOSE

Envision phase. Remember, the Speculate phase is Agile's answer to the Planning phase of the traditional Waterfall method. Much of the work done in the Speculate phase will resemble planning, but with an added level of flexibility and a more honest and anticipatory acknowledgment of the fact that calculations and even business goals are likely to change as the project proceeds.

When using the Agile methodology for software projects, iterations (Speculate, Explore, Adapt) usually last from two to six weeks. Hardware projects will usually have longer time frames. In either case, project costs and risks must be assessed and, when deciding on which features to incorporate into the project, the customer or end user should be consulted.

The selection of features is one of the most important parts of the Speculate phase. Many Agile users will use index cards or Post-it notes to categorize different types and statuses of features on a whiteboard. Features tend to fall into the following status categories:

New
These features have been established to support the current project.

Backlogged
These features are currently considered necessary for completion of the project but have not yet been developed. Should the project manager continue to deem them necessary, they will need to be assigned to a sprint at some point.

Incomplete
These features have already been through at least one iteration (Speculate, Explore, or Adapt) but will require more development. They will be moved to the backlog list during the following iteration.

In addition to assessing the time and resource commitments that will go into your features and outlining a delivery plan, it's also important during the Speculate phase to drill down on the unique risk assessments associated with your features. As explained in Chapter 4, the more complex the feature, the more risky it is thought to be.

To summarize, once the Speculate phase is finished and you are ready to move into the Explore phase, the team should have produced the following deliverables:

- An assessment of the features required to complete the project, along with their technical and personnel requirements
- An estimate of the amount of time or collective man-hours that will be required to develop each feature
- An assessment of the risks inherent in each feature
- A collection of significant milestones
- A release plan

The first time a team moves through the Speculate phase—immediately after the Envision phase—the time needed to complete the required speculation will be much greater. This is because the first Speculate phase requires the team to lay out their estimates and plan for the entire project front-to-back, just like they would if they were using a standard Waterfall approach. What makes Agile unique is that not only does it allot front-end planning time but it also institutes recurring planning times that happen at the beginning of every iteration, in the "Speculate" phase. After you complete the first major Speculate phase, the following Speculate phases can be accomplished in a shorter time period, because rather than speculating on the whole project, you'll only be speculating on a certain block of features to be developed in the next iteration. By instituting recurring, designated planning times, Agile allows projects to remain flexible and responsive to the changing needs of business.

During the initial Speculate phase, some Agile teams create *product roadmaps*, tools used to assess and visualize requirements, timetables, and task priority levels for a project. The product roadmap need not strictly conform to the constraints of limiting factors such as budget or personnel. While you should make estimates, you're free to make them quite broadly. All of these initial estimates and timetables will inevitably be clarified and changed as the project proceeds.

To illustrate (create) your product roadmap, use visual tools that are shareable, flexible, and simple. Many Agile teams simply use a whiteboard and sticky notes. You will arrange your proposed features for a project into groupings called "themes." Themes are macro-level requirements of the project. In our AR video game, a theme might be "game play" and would contain a multitude of game-play–related features. Another theme could be "rewards" and would handle how rewards would be distributed to players. Another theme might be "security" and would be devoted to protecting user data.

When developing your product roadmap, your team will begin by identifying the major themes of the project. In determining themes, and subsequently determining which features should be developed to support them, it's important that project stakeholders be involved as well as those who will be responsible for developing the product. The development of the product roadmap provides a space for important dialog between stakeholders and developers about end goals, strategies, resources, and limits of the project.

Once the main themes and features of your product have been identified, you will want to evaluate your features or assign "scores" for each feature using certain criteria. When scores are assigned, they should be made in a relative context with respect to the other features required for the project. This is why it's important to first get a broad view of the features you'll be developing, so that you'll know how to score them relative to one another.

The two principal scoring metrics used during the estimation process are value and effort. The product's stakeholder will be primarily responsible for scoring the value of various features, whereas the development team will be responsible for scoring the effort. An effective system for scoring features relative to one another can be found in the famous Fibonacci sequence. The Fibonacci sequence is the ordering of numbers whereby each successive number is the sum of the previous two: 1, 1, 2, 3, 5, 8, 13, 21, 34, 55, 89, 144, 233, etc. A feature with an effort score of 144 or 233 will be exceptionally challenging and time-intensive for the development team, whereas a feature with a score of 8 or 13 should go a lot quicker. Using the Fibonacci sequence to score features works, because it naturally accounts for the uncertainty inherent in quantifying the complexities posed by larger features; as features become more complex, it's more difficult to estimate the associated workload.[7]

When assessing value, a 144 or 233 would indicate an extremely valuable feature, and an 8 or 13 may be something the product could do without if need be. If your team is going to maintain a disciplined scoring process with clearly defined standards for various scoring thresholds, that's great. Don't worry about maintaining parity of scores, or similar distributions of scores between value and effort. Even if your value appraisers, for instance, tend to use scores lower on the Fibonacci sequence and your effort appraisers tend to use higher scores, it won't distort your analyses so long as the features are always scored relative to one another. If the scores in each category are applied with appropriate relativity, you can generate a new metric, called "relative priority," that will help you with prioritization of features.

The formula for relative priority is simply value/effort. As the value of the project goes up so does its relative priority. The relative priority

---

[7] Asmaier, February 20, 2012 (1:55 p.m.), comment on Stack Overflow (blog), http://stackoverflow.com/questions/9362286/why-is-the-fibonacci-series-used-in-agile-planning-poker.

will lower as the effort score climbs. As an example, let's say that our value appraisers tend to score features high—89, 144, etc.—and the effort appraisers score features lower: 8, 21, 34. When we attempt to use relative priority to compare various features, we will get useful comparisons, despite the fact that our value scores are high and our effort scores are low. They would also be usable if the reverse were the case (high effort scores, low value scores). They would even be usable if one or both of the scoring teams used a scale other than the Fibonacci sequence. All that matters is that the scores issued are consistently relative to other scores given. Consider the following three sample relative priority ratings:

89 (value score) /8 (effort score) = 11.13 (relative priority score)
144 (value score) /21 (effort score) = 6.86 (relative priority score)
144 (value score) /34 (effort score) = 4.24 (relative priority score)

Based on our calculation of relative priority score, the task valued at 89 should be higher priority than both tasks valued at 144. This is because the relative effort required is so low.

It's important to understand that attaining your relative priority rating should support, not define, how you prioritize your features in your product roadmap. There will certainly be factors to consider other than the relative priority rating. For example, if certain features cannot be developed before others are developed, or if you require access to specialized personnel for the development of specific features, then the team must account for these factors when prioritizing their work.

Understanding User Stories

One of the most important Agile tools that you'll create and reference in the Speculate phase and throughout the life cycle of an Agile project is the user story. A *user story* is a one- or two-sentence structured testimonial that provides a customer's perspective on the need for a product.

As a [fill in the blank], I want to [fill in the blank], so that [fill in the blank].

Let's suppose that our project is to develop an online job board for engineers. One of the user stories we use in our project might look like this:

As an [engineer looking for work online], I want to [browse employers who are looking for a specific skill], so that [I can reach prospective employers who have a specific need for the skills I provide].

Organizations using Agile often solicit user stories from all of their team members—anyone can contribute regardless of rank or experience—and then they record the user stories on index cards or Post-it notes, where they can be viewed by the whole team, discussed, organized, reconsidered, and reorganized.

What a user story does is allow the team to create a vision for their customer. The team will begin to envision what their customer's priorities are, what problems they have, and what their expectations are from services like those the team intends to provide. There's also a powerful double-checking utility inherent in the use of user stories. The last field of the standard user story is "so that," which should clearly define the customer's expectation. Let's return to our project example from Chapter 4, the AR game for the theme park. We said that one of the features we wanted was the ability of the player to earn experience points while playing the game that would make him more likely to win prizes. We might develop a user story that resembles the following:

As a [player of the game], I want to [see how many points I need to reach the next level], so that [I can work toward a specific prize].

We learn something in this user story. We learn that we can meet a valuable customer's need by showing him what prizes are available and may become available based on the level he's reached in the game. Since our user story explains that he wishes to work toward a specific prize, then, during our next Speculate phase, we might consider adding a feature that shows game players what prizes they currently qualify for as well as what prizes they'll qualify for after they reach the next level. We could use that same user story for another or multiple other features as well. We might add a feature that allows users to pick a prize they want at the beginning of the game and then receive updates throughout their gameplay detailing how close (or how far away) they are from earning their sought-after prize.

User stories are written throughout the course of the project life cycle. Some organizations host a user story writing workshop at the very beginning of the project, where all team members are invited and encouraged to participate. User stories are usually titled and ranked. A metric called *story points* can be used to separate the simpler stories from those that are more expansive and require complex evaluation and response. Just like the value and effort metrics used to rank features, story points may also be scored using the Fibonacci sequence. Just as with the scoring of features, scoring of user stories by way of "story points" will prove perpetually useful so long as the stories are scored relative to one another. Some user stories are particularly broad, something like this:

As a player of video games, I want to share my gaming experiences with my friends, so that we can have a fun way to keep in touch.

In the context of our AR theme park game, this user story would be considered epic, since it presumably would require a multitude of features to resolve. We'd have to set up a camera within the game app, a way to push the photo content through one or many social sharing APIs, and we'd have to have an EULA (End User License Agreement) created containing all the privacy and legal liability issues that our users would need to sign off on in order to use the feature.

User stories don't necessarily pertain only to normal use of the app. For example:

As a hacker, I want to exploit security vulnerabilities, so that I can access sensitive user data.

It's important to consider all potential interactions and interactors with the product, not just those for which the product is intended. In the above "hacker" example, the user story would be scored on the basis of how much work is required to ensure that the app is secure.

Using Performance Requirement Cards

Sometimes a function is required of a product, but the function can't simply be expressed as a feature. Our AR game, for example, will require a GPS feature that will report the user's geographic position to the game. In order for the game to work properly, it must be able to consistently track the user's position as he or she moves about the park; therefore, a performance requirement might be that the GPS report must be updated every five seconds.

fig. 10

Performance Requirement Card	
Requirement number:	17
Requirement name:	GPS update frequency
Performance criteria:	New GPS data must be incorporated into gameplay every 5 seconds
Complexity factor: (low, medium, high)	High
Acceptability point of measurement:	GPS update timelog and testing team report detail
Verified by:	Development lead

As shown in figure 10, the performance requirement is assigned a unique number and/or a unique name. The criteria for performance satisfaction are explained, and a complexity level is assigned. At the bottom of the card is a description of how the performance required is to be measured and by whom it's to be verified.

At the discretion of the team, some performance attributes may be notated by using an "acceptance test" that's written onto a feature card rather than a stand-alone performance requirement card. The key things to consider are whether the particular performance threshold needs an added level of independent visibility, whether it depends on multiple features, and whether the added detail of the performance requirement card—such as the identity of the verifying party and the "acceptability point of measurement"—is necessary for providing better visualization of project requirements.

Using Daily Meetings

Another important tool of the Speculate phase is regular structured meetings. Meetings in Agile have many names. Teams using the Scrum offshoot of Agile (see Chapter 9) refer to this daily meeting as the "Daily Scrum." Others refer to it as the "daily stand-up meeting," so named because the attendees are expected to stand on their feet for the duration of the meeting. The point is to ensure that the meetings don't drag on but retain a sharp, pointed focus on the issues of the day. During these meetings, each member of the development team is responsible for issuing a brief report. The format is something akin to the following:

Yesterday I worked on [state what was worked on yesterday].
Today I'll be working on [state what's to be worked on today].
My impediments are [state any impediments].

This format is designed to assure focus and brevity. As a general rule, stakeholders should not participate in the daily stand-up meeting, only developers. If stakeholders want to converse with developers, then they should seek them out after the meeting. You don't want long back-and-forths to take place during the team's daily stand-up meeting. The focus should be on ensuring that everyone is on the same page for the day's workload; it's not intended to be a forum for theoretical discussion or even for problem resolution. Now, that doesn't mean that team members shouldn't keep alert for reports of impediments that they may be able to help resolve. Just don't use the *meeting* to present your solutions. Instead, find the person after the meeting and help them resolve the impediment. If meeting participants frequently bring up issues that need immediate resolution, then, rather than attempting to resolve the issues or answer the questions right away, write the problems down on a special section of the whiteboard so that they may be resolved immediately following the meeting. Some Scrum teams institutionalize after-meeting problem solving by holding an optional "after-party" meeting following the daily stand-up. The brilliance of this model is that it prevents people from being stuck in a meeting when they've got work to do, but it gives people who need help a way to get it.

To ensure that the meeting proceeds in a timely manner, assign one team member to play the role of timekeeper and to crack the whip if someone begins to drone on for too long. The project lead (*product owner*) should not be running this meeting. An order should be established to determine which development team member reports first, and that order should be adhered to. Some teams like to switch the order of reporting every week or every day to keep things fresh, which is great so long as everyone is clear on the sequence and ready to jump in when it's their turn to report.

When participating in the daily stand-up as a product owner or a member of a development team, pay attention to the mood of the team.

Is it apathetic, cynical, energetic, optimistic? You don't need more than a few minutes of meeting time to get a good feel for team chemistry. You should also be able to ascertain whether the group is working at a pace appropriate for the tasks it's responsible for completing. If the *product backlog* continues to grow and the pace of issue-resolution and feature release is slow, then you'll need to figure out what's causing your team to underperform.

Depending on the size of your team and how closely they work together on a daily basis, you may be able to reduce the frequency of your stand-up meetings from daily to biweekly or once weekly. You may also consider having special meetings, usually on a less frequent basis, where you invite product stakeholders to get updated on the status of a project. When hosting these special meetings, consider allotting ten to twenty minutes of time at the end of the meeting specifically for stakeholders to ask questions.

Using Agile to Promote Flexibility of Pacing & Thought

Agile, in many ways, teaches us to think and to plan by means that accommodate the tools and technologies we use. Agile as a process has a built-in awareness of how impossible it is to build an entirely accurate or even usable front-end plan. In the past, project managers would be the ones responsible for determining exactly what would be required for a project and how long it would take, but now, with Agile, that responsibility is shared among the members of the development team. With Agile, the estimates offered for timelines, production schedules, and the like are in a constant and thoughtful state of flux. Thoughtful, because the system demands continuous evaluation, prioritization, and estimation. With Agile, better estimates are possible in successive iterations, because the team members are continuously amassing hands-on experience with the project. Meanwhile, the stakeholders and even customers benefit from more immediate exposure to finished, usable products.

The scope of an Agile project is defined by the features contained in the product backlog as well as newly added features. There's usually not a definitive number of features that you must have, nor is there a number which you must be careful not to surpass. By contrast, the cumulative expected duration of a given sprint should remain constant—each sprint should be of similar duration.

Measuring Sprint Velocity

When it comes to time management and measuring the pace of work, *sprint velocity* is one of the most important measurements in Agile. Velocity can be determined by averaging the story points resolved by a development team during a series of sprints. The number you're trying to get at is the number of story points that can be resolved during a given sprint. That's your velocity.

Note: Depending on who you ask, you can also measure sprint velocity in other ways, such as the cumulative effort ratings for the functions being developed.

Velocity can be used for a wide variety of business purposes. Let's say you're attempting to time the release of your product, so that it's up and running by a certain date, like opening day of the Olympic Games. You're building a software system for Olympic village—the temporary residences where Olympic athletes are housed—that will help make athletes aware of their competition schedules, transportation arrangements, and any other special factors that will ensure they report to their events on time. You can use velocity measurements to make certain the product is tested and ready to release by opening day. You do this by totaling all of the user story points that need to be resolved, and then determining how many sprints will be required at your current velocity. You may also use velocity to conform to budgetary requirements.

If your development team costs about $50,000 a week and your project budget is $500,000, then you'll need to determine how many sprints are possible in ten weeks (as you will have ten weeks before you go over budget on labor) and then use your sprint velocity to determine how many story points can be resolved during that time period. There are a multitude of other reasons that a project manager, stakeholder, or product owner may want to exert control over the development and release timelines. For instance,

- If a particular product needs to be scheduled for release at the beginning of a holiday season
- If a product needs to be released to market as soon as possible after it has demonstrated sufficient functionality
- If a product needs to be released at the same time as another organization (or another department within your organization) releases a complementary product
- If a product needs to be released at the same time as a competitor's product

In each of these scenarios the priorities set will be in accordance with business interests, and the Agile system allows product developers to respond more predictably and in a coherent way given the specified time frame.

Things can get a little tricky if you attempt to guess your team's velocity before they begin work. Velocity is best measured after the team has had a chance to complete a few sprints. If you're working with a deadline or within a budget, then you'll need to gradually focus the project as it proceeds through development. Don't attempt to do all of the planning at the beginning—remember, we're using Agile, not Waterfall. If you wander and explore and speculate before you determine the way forward, then you'll fare better in the end.

Chapter Recap

- The Agile Project Management Framework's second phase, Speculate, is focused on the development of piecemeal project components (features) by way of short, iterative bursts of work (sprints).

- Product roadmaps can be used to outline the requirements for a project.

- Feature production can be qualified and organized using basic scoring systems.

- Performance requirement cards and daily "stand-up" meetings are used in the Speculate phase to assess project progress.

- Sprint velocity can be used to quantify and manage the work pace of an Agile team.

| 5 |

The Explore Phase

In This Chapter
- Details of Agile's Explore Phase
- The Role of the Project Manager in the Explore Phase
- Self-Organizing Teams
- Plan, Do, Check, Adjust

The Explore phase refers to the beginning of actual production. With Agile, you'll get into the Explore phase much quicker than you would with Waterfall. Explore is not meant to be interpreted as reckless experimentation, throwing a bunch of ideas out there and seeing what sticks. Quite the opposite actually, the Explore phase is meant to efficiently and steadily uncover possibilities for innovation in a cost-effective manner. Agile guru and author of *Agile Project Management: Creating Innovative Products*, Jim Highsmith, asserts four technical practices that keep costs low while expanding possibilities for innovation: Simple Design, Frequent Integration, Ruthless Testing, and Opportunistic Refactoring.[8]

Simple Design
This practice asserts that the design of a given feature should be pursued with simplicity in mind. If you're familiar with the phrase "dead-end code," then you know how difficult it can be to rework programming work that was complexly constructed, even when

---

[8] Jim Highsmith, *Agile Project Management: Creating Innovative Products* (Upper Saddle River, NJ, Addison-Wesley), 2010.

the ultimate function served by the programming isn't itself highly complex. Highsmith recommends a process whereby a system is first designed to solve a problem in as simple a manner as possible, and afterwards the solvent system is refactored to conform to "design patterns." Design patterns are norms that have been proven reliable over time and pave the way for ease of integration into a larger product. A simple and standardized system also makes it easier and less expensive to conduct experiments and to adapt to changing factors. Together, these two advantages allow for the utmost probability of significant innovation.

Frequent Integration

Up until now we've discussed user stories and features as individual component pieces of a product and have not addressed the issue of integration. Highsmith urges Agile teams to adopt the practice of frequent integration on the basis that it's highly preferable to developing an integration scheme only after a smattering of component functions are already up and running. One may wonder whether pursuing frequent integration may distort velocity, presuming that integration will become more and more complex as the project expands. The truth is that it does just the opposite. Being proactive and systematic on integration issues minimizes the footprint. Many development teams use integration control systems and policies, whereby new code (in the case of programming) is always submitted to an established integration framework, which tests and analyzes the code, facilitating expedient integration with the larger system.

Ruthless Testing

The overarching theory behind ruthless testing is that the work will go quicker and the product will be better if a high standard of product quality is maintained throughout the development process. Each sprint should culminate in the creation of features that correctly and reliably execute their functions. Each feature should be thought of as a mini-product with independent intrinsic value. When defects are identified and weeded out early, a much cleaner, smoother work environment is created. Changes can be made and experiments can be conducted at low cost. Furthermore, development team members, if made to interact and work with a consistently tested product, will have a clearer idea of the product's ultimate capabilities. If testing is not conducted regularly, aggressively, and accurately, then development team members are left in the unenviable position of making assumptions about various underlying product components ("Assuming we get all the bugs out of component A, component B should work fine"). When ruthless testing is the norm, these verifications are instant ("Because we ruthlessly tested component A, we can now test component B and verify for certain that it works as intended"). Automated testing at regular intervals and using many varieties of tests are the key components of ruthless testing.

Opportunistic Refactoring

This is about not being satisfied merely because a product works. Developers must also be on the lookout for opportunities to improve the product's internal strengths, such as the efficiency of its programming, in order to ensure that the product can be deployed in diverse settings and can be readily updated and expanded. The refactoring protocol should always include a test at the end to ensure that no change to the design caused a material change in performance.

When you consider all of Highsmith's recommended technical practices together, then you will see how they coordinate and reinforce one another. It's easier to integrate various features of a product if they've been constructed following a simple and standardized protocol. It's easier to test a product if it's been effectively integrated. And it's easier to refactor a product if you're able to immediately test its ability to retain its functionality after the refactoring is complete.

During the Explore phase, the development team will rely on the daily stand-up meetings to coordinate work. As we discussed in the previous chapter, the daily stand-up meetings should be kept short and should be used for reporting and observing, not problem resolution.

If you're in the role of a project manager, use the stand-up meetings to listen and observe. You should be on the lookout for impediments that could be preventing development team members from handling their assignments efficiently and accurately. Developers who are engaged with their work and feel as if they're making progress will be more likely to demonstrate a high level of confidence and pride when reporting. Developers who are frustrated or who aren't as focused as they need to be may not be very forthcoming about their work and may give off an air of disinterest or annoyance at the meeting despite its special focus on being short and to the point.

The ending of an Explore phase is marked by the delivery of tested features. This is usually packaged around the ending of a sprint. On some occasions, however, an Explore phase must come to an end before new deliverables have been produced. For example, if a development team exceeds its time allotment for the Explore phase without producing the planned deliverables, then it's time for them to proceed to the Adapt phase where they'll assess what went wrong and reset the course.

Leadership through Service

Unlike the traditional, Waterfall approach to project management, where leadership exerts its will from the top down, in Agile Project Management a great multitude of leadership faculties are defined and driven by the development team. For instance, it is up to the development team to determine the priorities of the various features and to estimate how long each feature will take to develop. The project manager is there primarily to remove any obstacles that might stand in the way of optimal performance by the team.

Scrum, one of the most popular Agile methodologies, defines a project management role called a "Scrum Master." It is in this role that the unique leadership principles of Agile Project Management are codified. Many discussions of Agile use ScrumMaster as a term that's interchangeable with project manager. Other discussions try to delineate a difference between the two. The reason for this confusion is that the uniquely Agile roles, such as ScrumMaster, are an outgrowth of the traditional project manager role. In some organizations the title "project manager" is retained, even though this person, when working on Agile projects, acts effectively as a ScrumMaster. In other organizations, the two roles are delineated, and while the ScrumMaster focuses on the Agile process and plays the role of the "servant leader," the formal project manager is in charge of financial monitoring of the project and maintaining communications with the stakeholders. Many in the Agile-friendly communities refuse to use the term "project manager" for any team member if the team, as a whole, is pursuing Agile Project Management. This hostile sentiment toward the term "project manager" comes from the term's association with the more traditional methodologies of project management. Hard-core Agile proponents are pursuing a major reinvention in the art of project management, and this includes a reinvention of language.

Regardless of whether the leader of an Agile team is considered the "project manager," the "ScrumMaster," or anything else, it's important that someone play the role of master facilitator (servant leader) for the Agile team. In some setups the organization elects to use both a ScrumMaster and a project manager for the same project. The ScrumMaster is put in charge of overseeing Agile methodologies, while the general project manager takes care of stakeholder relations and may also oversee more traditional, Waterfall-style initiatives when needed. If the processes used for a particular project are fairly well defined, then a Waterfall approach may prove optimal. If the project requires more innovative, outside-the-box thinking, then the Agile methodology will grant the development team more flexibility.

In short, the principal responsibilities of an Agile project manager/ScrumMaster/servant manager are the following:

1. **Facilitate communication between team members.** It falls on the Agile project manager to set up a time for the daily stand-up or Scrum meetings and to ensure that team members are present and participating. Especially in highly technical projects, getting people to meaningfully interact on a regular basis is an important and challenging job.

2. **Clear impediments.** The last item reported by the development team members during a daily stand-up meeting is the impediments they are encountering in their current roles. A good Agile project manager listens to the concerns expressed and makes every effort to clear impediments to ensure optimal performance by the team.

3. **Coach.** The Agile project manager is charged with safeguarding morale and identifying pockets of anxiety or despair. If an employee (or group of employees) isn't buying into the system, then the system won't function as effectively.

4. **Support team decisions.** The role of the Agile project manager is not to make decisions for the group but to facilitate the group's ability to make its own decision and then to allow things to take

their course based on that decision. Even if the Agile project manager doesn't agree with the group's decision, he should still strive to support it. Keep in mind that the Agile methodology is designed so that mistakes can be made throughout the product development process. It's expected that you, as the project manager, will be wrong on some occasions and that your team will be wrong on some occasions. The Agile approach is to learn as much as can be learned from mistakes. If you were against the idea from the beginning, then see if you can learn anything else from a mistake other than what you already knew or suspected might happen.

5. **Watch for team stressors.** The Agile Project Management system can be intense, especially when the sprints commence and feature development begins. If a project is ten weeks long, for example, weeks two to nine are likely to be the most intense because they will occupy the bulk of feature design time. Keep an eye out for stressed team members and develop ways to moderate the workload. Try to pace your weeks so that for every two to three weeks of intense work, there's one week that's a little more laid back.

6. **Secure resources.** The Agile project manager is responsible for ensuring that the team members have all of the resources necessary to do their jobs. Resources may include various types of information, such as customer data or marketing data. The types of software and hardware that will aid in work on the project are, of course, important resources. There are also intangible resources, such as training courses, curricula, and tests, as well as access to specialized personnel, subject matter experts, designers, consultants, etc.

The Power of the Self-Organizing Team

Rather than relying on a project manager who acts like a taskmaster, the Agile system opts for a project manager who acts like a servant. The team is the entity that has ultimate authority and ownership over the project. Among other things, self-organized Agile teams assess their productive capacity and define their sprint targets based on requests from the product owner. The product owner is the Agile team member who, more so than anyone else, knows about what the product is and does. The product owner is also the tie that binds together the development team, the customer, and the business stakeholders.

The product owner's responsibility is to communicate to the development team what the product needs (this is often done via the collaborative recording of user stories) and the development team will be able to parse out the various features required, determine how much time it will take for each feature, and then incorporate that time allotment into a planned sprint. A self-organizing team is also proactive when it comes to communicating with one another. Rather than relying on emails or waiting for a higher-up to facilitate communication, the team members identify necessary communications and speak face-to-face with other team members whenever possible.

A self-organized team will generally produce a better product than a team that's being driven by a boss. An emphasis on shared ownership over the product, proactive communications, and self-determined task management all contribute to optimized results. As a project manager or ScrumMaster, you will want to do all you can to vividly portray the potential advantages of self-organization: greater personal autonomy, a more meaningful work experience, and the development of a potentially ground-breaking product.

There's certainly an art that goes into the cultivation of a successful self-organizing team. Sometimes, once you feel that self-organization has been established, it's difficult to assess the factors that were responsible, and therefore it's difficult to reliably replicate them. Nonetheless, being part of a self-organizing team allows you to look around and observe some of the elements that keep the team in a positive flow. Then when you try to replicate that team dynamic for a future project, at least you'll know what it is you're looking for. One of the key features of a strong self-organizing team is the fluidity of leadership. The role of the leader will pass naturally from person to person. The team members will become keen and sensitive to opportunities to be good leaders, as well as opportunities to be good followers. Since there is no formal boss or taskmaster, no one needs to guard their ego, but can instead allow the best ideas and solutions to surface amid the group. Good team members in a self-organizing team are continuously putting out current and useful information. This is primarily done in the form of work reports given during the daily stand-up meeting. But it's also expected that team members will actively participate throughout the duration of a project. For interpersonal conflicts or arguments, the local resolution is strongly preferred. The team itself should be the principal adjudicator for problems that arise within it.

Handling Issues within Self-Organizing Teams

For disagreements that arise concerning how to proceed on various tasks or features, or how to accurately score a user story or feature, team members must strive to detach themselves from the need to be "right." The beauty of Agile is that mistakes are expected and will always add new information to the system (and to the team), even if they fail to offer sustainable solutions. Furthermore, the evaluation structure used by Agile evaluates the performance of the team as a collective unit. There will be no individual performance reports following any given project. The whole team is going to be either right or wrong together.

One potential sign of trouble is when you notice that a small group of team members appear to be driving the project and the rest appear disinterested, just along for the ride. These organic micro-oligarchies, though natural, are certainly not preferred. One way to introduce a fresh dynamic into the team is to mix up the various roles. Part of the beauty of Agile is that team members are not relegated to one particular job, but are expected to be willing to jump into roles that may be outside of their comfort zones or areas of expertise.

Problems may also arise if the project's stakeholders or customers are not regularly available to collaborate with the development team. The input, especially of the customer, is critical, since they must ultimately be satisfied with the resulting product. Another potential problem comes when the development team is ready to employ the Agile methodology, but the stakeholders or customers aren't familiar with Agile and are taken aback by its lack of a hierarchical structure. In these situations, educating stakeholders on the basics of Agile philosophy and soliciting their routine interaction with the project are likely to yield favorable results.

In order to ensure necessary participation by all involved parties, many Agile teams adopt the Plan, Do, Check, Adjust (PDCA) method of production.

fig. 11

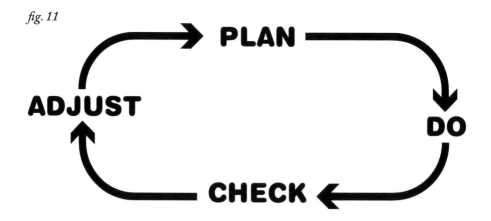

Plan

During the "plan" phase of the cycle, the Agile team assesses its objectives, expectations, and potential problems. It is also useful to consider testing endeavors during the planning phase. Find out what information and real-time feedback your team will require in order to develop the best possible product, and structure your planning accordingly.

Do

The "do" phase is about implementing the planned course of action and retrieving accurate data that will inform the next two steps of the process, "check," and "adjust."

Check

The "check" phase provides room for Agile teams to assess the compatibility of the "plan" and "do" phases. Did the results brought about by the "do" phase reflect the goals established in the "plan" phase? Did the results exceed expectations or fall short? Was the plan carried out properly in the "do" phase or were there deviations? As a project proceeds through several iterations, having a log that documents several plans and the results of their corresponding executions can come in handy. Large-scale patterns can be used to further perfect the process. Information recorded in the "check" phase can be shared with project stakeholders along with proposals for process improvements, which constitute the next phase of the PDCA cycle, "adjust."

Adjust

The "adjust" phase is about continually establishing higher standards for the project. Over the course of several iterations, the goals established in the "plan" phase, the efficiency of the "do" phase, and the rigorousness of the "check" phase should become more enhanced.

If your product stakeholders remain plugged in to your PDCA process, then you will notice a continual improvement in quality that will meet and often exceed stakeholder expectations. In many ways the "adjust" portion of the PDCA cycle is a microcosm of the Adapt phase of the Agile Project Management Framework, discussed in the following chapter.

Chapter Recap

- The Agile Project Management Framework's third phase, Explore, is focused on uncovering opportunities for innovation.

- Project managers in Agile don't manage so much as facilitate, in accordance with the will of a "self-organizing" team.

| 6 |

The Adapt Phase

In This Chapter
- Details of Agile's Adapt Phase
- Obtaining Continual, Useful Feedback

Going back to our example of an augmented reality game taking place in the environment of a theme park, imagine that our Agile team had planned and attempted to work toward a gaming interface that required the players to aim their mobile devices at the theme park's roller coasters as they were in motion, following the path of the train along the track and earning points (in the game) for doing so. The product owner was enthusiastic about this particular feature because it would give park patrons something fun and rewarding to do while waiting in line. Now, let's say that for any variety of reasons, the use of live roller coasters in the AR gaming environment wasn't working out. The team had already been through a dozen or so "do" phases of the PDCA cycle, they had gone through a dozen or so "adjusts," and still no dice. But at the end of the sprint, the Agile team, rather than deeming the project a failure, pursues a holistically revised outlook on the nature of the problem at hand. Recognizing that the root concern of the product owner is providing patrons with a more enjoyable experience while waiting in line, the Agile team does not declare the endeavor a failure but instead speculates on a way by which the project can be productively "adjusted." One idea is to use the game's GPS overlay to concentrate more points of interest into line-waiting areas. Perhaps key virtual artifacts, necessary to complete certain objectives within the game, can only be accessed just shy of the boarding areas for popular rides. Therefore, gamers ultimately must ride certain rides in order to obtain their desired in-game collectibles. Another Agile team member suggests that the points of interest be dynamic and alterable, so that adjusting them may drive patrons to certain rides or to other sections of the park. Less popular rides might contain more valuable virtual artifacts, contributing to the balancing out of line-waiting times across attractions.

Though we weren't able to attain what we sought to attain during our initial Speculate phase, we chose to Adapt rather than to fail. And we were rewarded by value-adding alternatives that the technical staff, product owner, and all stakeholders feel comfortable with.

The Adapt phase takes place at the end of each sprint and centers on a comparison of what was delivered versus what was planned. There will, in most cases, be certain discrepancies between the plan and the result, and the Adapt phase is used to make changes and offer new suggestions. The Adapt phase is part of the perpetual Speculate, Explore, Adapt iteration; therefore, multiple Adapt phases may take place during the course of a given project. It's important that customers and stakeholders be involved in the Adapt phases, as there may be a need to discuss substantial changes to the project. It's also important that any new business needs be articulated to the Agile team before they revert back to the Speculation phase. For example, if our theme park executives have recently come to the decision that they need to attract more customers to their carnival game midway, then they will want to inform our Agile team to concentrate more points of interest on the midway. The theme park executives may have recently struck a deal with a new entertainment studio and will be obtaining licensure for a new portfolio of characters. Rather than "Pokefriends," the business now wants our Agile team to design its game using characters from "Dragon Warriors."

A successful Agile team will track the lessons learned and changes made across several successive Adapt phases. Doing so will provide the team with a process improvement meta-analysis. The team members will begin to get a sense of one another's strengths, weaknesses, and abilities to be flexible and adapt. The Adapt phase may include a shuffling of technology, responsibilities, and/or personnel. Depending on the analysis of the team, features and processes may be added or taken away. The contents and planned durations of upcoming sprints may be adjusted. Team members may be shuffled around. The Adapt phase may also include a critical review of the daily stand-up meetings. What might be done to make these meetings more helpful and more efficient? Speak now or hold your peace until after the next sprint.

While learning from your shortcomings is key, it's also important to take notice of what you've done right. The Adapt phase provides a chance to celebrate big accomplishments, such as the surpassing of milestones established during the Speculate phase.

Note: If your team is using the Scrum methodology, post–Sprint "Adapt" assessments are commonly referred to as "Sprint Retrospectives."

The Human Factor

Project managers have a lot of responsibilities including risk assessments, reporting, and fostering communication between team members. It's also incumbent upon the project manager to regularly assess the mental and physical well-being of the Agile team members. Agile can be an intense, fast-paced working method (they're called "sprints" for a reason), and people get tired. For project managers, the Adapt phase can be used to assess the morale and well-being of team members and to take action as appropriate; for example, a project manager may decide to excuse a team member from a certain sprint. The excused team member may use the time away from the project to take a vacation or to tend to company affairs outside the project. Some

Agile teams prefer to keep team members engaged only in the team's central project so long as it's still in development, the idea being that you're metaphorically locked in a room together, all you have is each other, and you need to focus all of your energy on supporting your team in your struggle for freedom, which of course is gained by completion of the project. The other potential problem with changing your team members too much is that it can make it more difficult to calculate "velocity" (see Chapter 5).

A Culture of Continuous Feedback

To nurture successful and perpetually fruitful Adapt phases, an Agile project manager must know how to elicit useful feedback. Successful project managers will ask pertinent questions and facilitate meaningful dialogs between team members. The acquisition of useful feedback should be continuous and should not be relegated only to the Adapt phases. Building a culture of continuous feedback is actually easier than you might think. Much of the Agile structure inadvertently limits room for continuous feedback. Daily stand-up meetings are designed to be quick and to the point, unencumbered by protracted theoretical discussions or general complaints. Sprints are designed to be fast-paced and focused, not contemplative. Therefore, if you provide an ongoing forum for your team members to provide general feedback, then they'll likely take advantage of it. A physical feedback box can work well in this respect. You may also be able to leverage your online collaboration tools (see Chapter 4) to solicit feedback. Employees may candidly record and deposit their thoughts on various matters without having to offer immediate solutions. Complaints and suggestions are reviewed during the Adapt phase, and are hopefully paired with viable remedies. Using a feedback box or a similar setup allows your Agile team to concurrently generate continuous feedback while also capitalizing on the rigorous focus inherent in the Agile Project Management method. The content of the feedback box will also inspire new and innovative ideas from the team. In many cases, it won't be feasible to immediately implement all of the ideas generated. The team will have to prioritize the importance of the ideas in the Adapt phase and decide which ones to incorporate into the next sprint, which ones to add to the product backlog, and which ones to disregard. The Scrum team as a whole should be involved in the prioritization process, either through voting or by some other means.

Chapter Recap

- The Agile Project Management Framework's third phase, Adapt, emphasizes a responsive flexibility that welcomes new opportunities for adding value and new definitions of success.

- Though the interpretation of feedback is technically assigned to the Adapt phase, all efforts should be made to collect continuous feedback throughout the life cycle of a project.

| 7 |

The Close Phase

After the Adapt phase, the project will either revert back to the Speculate phase, or, if the project has attained its end point, then it will be moved into the Close phase. Project end points can be established for various reasons, some good, some not so good. If all of the features scheduled for development have been completed, then the project has come to an end and can enter the Close phase. The project may also enter the Close phase for administrative reasons, for instance if it exceeds its budget and fails to acquire more funds. The project may end due to a changing business need. For example, the theme park we're working for may decide that an AR game is just too much of a legal liability—their insurance bill is already expensive enough. And on some occasions, projects come to an end simply because time runs out on a time-sensitive project. If my Agile team is creating a dynamic voter database that will help us turn out voters on election day, that project may not be viable after the election is over and may therefore be shut down.

The central function of the Close phase is to ensure that all lessons learned from the closure (and hopefully completion) of the project are categorized and reintegrated into the collective knowledge of the business or organization. Much like a retrospective meeting is held during the Adapt phase after the completion of each sprint, a more broadly scoped retrospective meeting is held at the conclusion of a project. This broad assessment of the project, and the perspective it brings, is unique to the Close phase and what really makes that phase worthwhile. Some Agile teams may also produce a retrospective report or document detailing the key lessons learned. The attendance at a retrospective meeting may include a larger subsection of interested parties, including not just stakeholders and customers, but executive leadership as well. Outside parties may be invited to attend these meetings if warranted by circumstance. Since new eyes will be on the project during the Close phase, new ideas may also be generated and new features may be called for. Existing features on the backlog list may be green-lit as well. Part of the customary retrospective is a review of the features that were on the backlog but never made it to production. If, for instance, a project is brought to the Close phase after exceeding its budget, certain backlogged features may still be resurrected or rolled into a new project, depending on the wishes of the stakeholders. It's also possible for a participant in the retrospective process to come up with a must-have idea for a new feature, which, again, either results in the resurrection of the project or the new feature being rolled into a new project.

In other retrospective meetings, the stakeholders may decide that the features on the backlog may simply be disregarded. Another possibility is that the backlogged features may be wait-listed and perhaps implemented in the future depending on the performance of the product as is.

During the Close phase, project-specific administrative tasks should be resolved before the team disbands and information becomes decentralized. Vendors must be paid. Accounts receivable must be collected. Team members must be made aware of their next assignments. A monitoring infrastructure should be erected to track the ongoing impact of the project on business needs. The organization as well as the project manager and team members are going to want to know the extent to which their efforts made a difference.

Transition Management

It's the responsibility of the project manager to ensure that team members are clear about when their work on the project is complete. As a project winds down it's not uncommon for some team members to be excused before others, depending on their responsibilities. The project manager should ensure that team members whose work is complete transition smoothly to their next role within the organization, facilitating this transfer by maintaining adequate communication with both the team members and their new managers. Given that most projects require several months to complete, the transition period can be emotionally jarring for team members, so be on the lookout for signs of stress and strive to be accommodating.

The Importance of Celebration

Agile guru Jim Highsmith, when describing the Close phase, says projects should end with a celebration.[9] Having a team celebration gives everyone a chance to appreciate all they've accomplished during the project. The Agile model is built on iterative bursts of hard, focused work, so it's only appropriate to party like there's no tomorrow once the work is complete. Celebrating the ending of a project will also instill in your team a sense of closure, a feeling that all their hard work was vindicated.

During the celebration event, if possible, ensure that team members are recognized for extraordinary accomplishments made during the course of the project. In addition to recognizing individual accomplishments,

---

[9] Jim Highsmith, "An Agile Project Management Model," *TechTarget.com*, accessed on 9/7/16, http://media.techtarget.com/searchEnterpriseLinux/downloads/04_Highsmith.pdf.

your Close phase celebration should include an acknowledgment of the team's success with the Agile methodology. It may be helpful to host an Agile debriefing session before your celebration where the team can discuss their perception of the framework over the course of the project. Where might the process be improved? Where and when did the process seem most useful?

Chapter Recap

- The Agile Project Management Framework's third phase, Close, is concerned with assimilating all knowledge gained from the project into the overall organizational intelligence.

- During the Close phase, project managers should ensure a healthy transition of team members into new projects.

| 8 |

The Canon of Agile Methodologies

In This Chapter
- Popular Variations of Agile

Variations of Agile

As stated in the preceding chapter, there are different sub-approaches within the Agile system. These are either derived from theories that existed before the Agile system was officially initiated, or they are the work of individual proponents. Some of them may, therefore, resemble earlier project management paradigms. This hereditary succession or adaptation is not a new phenomenon in project or business management. Since the inception of project management, there has been a substantial degree of intermixing and synthetic progression. This chapter does not purport to be an exhaustive discussion of all the available approaches under the Agile heading.

These sub-approaches are sometimes referred to as "flavors," a term taken from the software programming environment. The term is an indication of the distinctions that exist in order for a program to meet variable needs, such as those of users who rely on different operating systems or have other preferences.

Trying to assess which approach will best suit an organization requires a deep awareness of a project's specific nature and precise application. Research into the issue is necessary. No matter how positive other people's remarks may be about a specific variation of Agile, each project facilitator needs to compare it with their situation in order to determine whether it is a suitable course of action.

This list presents five of the most important variations in use today. They are not listed in order of importance or prevalence of use. As a general guideline, project managers are advised to observe described principles and established practices in order to evaluate each approach in relation to their common tasks. Ultimately, no project is ever any more successful than the commitment, hard work, and expertise of its team.

Scrum

This is the method most often mentioned in Agile literature. It is perhaps one of the best examples to highlight as an illustration of how Agile operates. Its internal processes, terminology, and style of team management are an accurate and transparent demonstration of how Agile functions and the philosophy that it entails. One of the first proponents of Agile, Ken Schwaber, was involved in the initial formulation of the Scrum method.

The word *scrum* is taken from the sport of rugby. For those who are unfamiliar with this sport, it is played by fifteen players on each team and closely resembles American football. The scrum is a movement engaged in by both teams, during which eight players on each side (the heaviest, most physically imposing members) pack together and push against their opponents in a collective effort.

But scrum isn't the only piece of rugby terminology in the system. There is also the "kick-off meeting," during which the project is discussed for the first time by the project team, in order to ascertain what the goals are and how they are going to be achieved. During this meeting, the *product backlog* is established. This is the tool used to keep track of the work that needs to be done, which is essentially what the customer desires from the initiative (the scope). The customer is defined, and their expectations are discerned in the form of "user stories."

In our AR game example, the theme park attendee would be the customer. And here are some examples of user stories:

- I want to earn, track, and redeem points for playing this game.
- I want to share my in-game achievements with my friends on Facebook.
- I want my gameplay options to expand as I progress through the game.

The iterations (stages) within the project are known as "sprints," and they are essentially the same as sprints used in the broader context of Agile. In each sprint, backlog items are selected and resolved, while new items that arise are placed on the product backlog to be addressed during future sprints.

Once a sprint is complete, the finished stage of the project is presented to the customer for their assessment and feedback, which will be used to add items to the product backlog and define further sprints. What is critical to realize about this example is that the game players (customers) may decide that they want different things during the course of successive releases of the game. Customers may find that features they thought they wanted actually detract from their experience, while features that didn't poll well in feedback logs prove quite popular in the real world. At these junctures, data from past projects of a similar nature may also prove helpful.

A sprint or "iteration" should not last more than four weeks. Sometimes it may be as short as one week. Regardless of the sprint's duration, it should culminate in the production of something of value for the end user (customer), even if it does not yield the ultimately desired outcome.

At the start of each sprint, team members hold a "sprint planning meeting." If this is not the first sprint, the meeting will be combined with a "sprint review meeting," which focuses on the preceding sprint. The targeted outcome for a particular sprint, the Sprint Goal, is established during the planning meeting.

At the start of each day, there is also a "daily stand-up meeting." This meeting typically does not last longer than fifteen minutes, and the members present are required to remain standing for its duration. This is supposed to symbolize and engender the sense of immediacy, alertness, and quick response that the system incorporates. In Scrum, this meeting is known as the Daily Scrum, and it is used to plan the next twenty-four hours of activity. During the Scrum, the following questions have to be answered:

- What did I do yesterday that was material to the Sprint Goal?
- What am I going to do today that is material to the Sprint Goal?
- Is there anything stopping us from reaching the Sprint Goal?

fig. 12

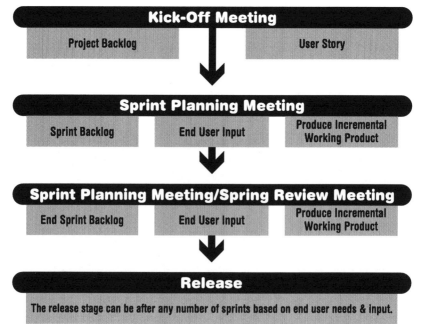

The backlog concept can be applied to either the sprint or the release, which is the eventual delivery of the ultimate product. During the course of the project or sprint, a Burndown Chart is used to track progress at each level. This is a graph that descends in its trajectory, marking project or sprint progress as proportional to the passage of time. The Task Board is used to promote awareness of the project in its entirety, from the user stories through the iterations to the finished stages. It is an invaluable tool that organizes and tracks tasks that have been initiated, are in progress, and have been completed. In conjunction with the Burndown Chart and the user stories, the Task Board provides a "one-stop shop" of vital information for the Scrum project team.

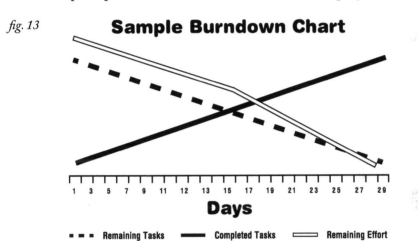

fig. 13

Sample Burndown Chart

Days

1 3 5 7 9 11 12 13 15 17 19 21 23 25 27 29

■ ■ ■ Remaining Tasks   ▬▬ Completed Tasks   ▭▭ Remaining Effort

fig. 14

SAMPLE TASK BOARD

STORY	NOT STARTED	STARTED	IN PROGRESS	DONE
USER STORY 1	H	F	B	A
	I	G	D	C
USER STORY 2	J			
	K		E	

The team in a Scrum project consists of three roles. These are:

- Product Owner
- ScrumMaster
- Development Team members

The Product Owner is the manager of the process. However, he or she does not micromanage the people who work on the project. The workers are left largely to manage themselves. Instead, the Product Owner takes responsibility for the list of backlog items, making sure that everyone knows what is on it and what each item represents. Sometimes they partially delegate this function to the Development Team. It is important to note that the Product Owner is a single person, not a management team.

The ScrumMaster is the person whose role is devoted to the implementation of the project management system itself. They need to be well acquainted with the Scrum (Agile) paradigm and be able to convey its practice and ideology to other staff members. They liaise with both the Product Owner and the Development Team in order to ensure that the Scrum system operates as it should.

The Development Team is typically small, although preferably not fewer than three members. It has no internal hierarchy or titles, other than Developer. It is self-managing, that is, no other person provides instructions on how to meet the backlog objectives. The Team comprises all the necessary expertise, and it accomplishes the required level and nature of activity each day. It is, therefore, cross-functional.

The outputs of the Scrum process, such as the backlog list and the product increments, are known as its artifacts.

This discussion of Scrum reveals certain terms and principles that are generic to all of the Agile sub-approaches. For the descriptions that follow, the reader can simply refer back to this discussion of Scrum in order to compare and understand them, even though the terms and the internal procedures used in each methodology may not be the same.

Lean

Lean is a business management philosophy employed and made prominent by the Toyota Motor Corporation. It is sometimes referred to as Toyotism or the Toyota Production System. Since the process must take place as quickly as possible, its priority is to ensure that the entire manufacturing process, from the supplier network to the end user, entails no wasted resources or time. It is an organizational strategy that aims at minimum expense and shortest possible duration with high levels of customer satisfaction.

Applying Lean to Agile is a natural management progression in enterprises that already make use of the former. It is an interesting approach, and it has some apparent advantages and snags.

On the plus side, the use of cross-functional teams enables less outlay of expertise. This is seen as a form of waste in the Lean and Six Sigma management paradigms, so the more fully staff is utilized, the better. Because Lean minimizes the costs of the project, it also allows for a greater return on investment (ROI), or a more substantial output on the customer's available budget.

On the other hand, Lean also requires constant monitoring of the project. It is sometimes based on statistical or other methods of assessment, and this necessitates the absorption of productivity time by what is essentially an administrative function. Project managers will need to decide whether the reduced expenses occasioned by the implementation of Lean are justified by the additional burden of work that it entails. This, coupled with the statistical analysis foundation of Lean, makes the pairing of Lean and Agile inappropriate for many product development projects. Lean is best applied to continuous processes (manufacturing or otherwise) while Agile harnesses the incremental production method to produce customer-tailored results.

Crystal

Crystal is another sub-approach that was devised by one of the original seventeen composers of the Agile philosophy, Alistair Cockburn. Cockburn still maintains a website on the methodology, and he states the following three underlying principles in his approach to software development (or any other project):

- **Human-powered**: maximizing the potential of each person on the project team (people-centric as opposed to other-centric)
- **Ultralight**: the least possible administration and auxiliary activities, regardless of project size or scope
- **Stretch-to-fit**: always start out with a little less than you need and expand it to requirements (prevents depletion or "cutting away")

(http://www.alistair.cockburn.us)

These principles reflect the Agile Manifesto (see Chapter 2), and in the case of the third principle, also a Lean aspect. It is no surprise that Cockburn lists reading matter on his site that is also found on the Japanese Just-In-Time (JIT) business management system.

Crystal is not one specific methodology, but rather a "family" or group of business methods. This is a source of criticism, since many methods are not mutually interchangeable and cannot be switched during the course of a project. While Crystal places a strong priority on the testing of a product under development (something which has always been a part of software design), it is not always feasible to have a team member dedicated to that activity in every team. In fact, this requirement may start to breach the second, "ultralight," principle.

One of the primary focuses of the Crystal set of methodologies, however, is that it is "human-powered," something also emphasized in the Agile Manifesto.

DSDM

The Dynamic Systems Development Method (DSDM) is an older system that has been adopted into the Agile stable. It uses several techniques to render the product according to loose Agile principles (that is, it is incremental and iterative). Some specific DSDM tactics include the following:

- MoSCoW Prioritization
- Timeboxing

(http://www.dsdm.org)

MoSCoW Prioritization refers to the method of identifying priorities in the project by using the concepts Must, Should, Could, and Won't. Timeboxing is related to the emphasis on establishing the desired quality, expense, and time frame of the project at its initiation, in keeping with the Agile approach. This method determines a specific time period (called a time box) for individual planned activities and focuses on meeting smaller, attainable deadline goals.

fig. 15

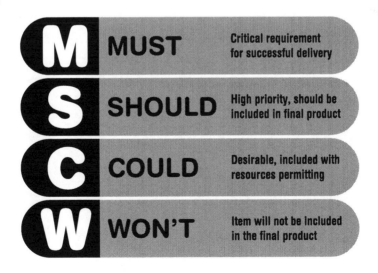

Like Crystal, the concentration on quality in DSDM requires a member of each team to function as a tester. At the same time, DSDM is designed to be the result of development and input by businesspeople in a business environment, so it regards value as the most important objective of the project. MoSCoW Prioritization allows both the project team and the end user to determine which requirements of the product are essential and which are optional, so that the end user does not have unrealistic expectations about what the technology is capable of or what is possible on the available budget of time or money. Timeboxing is merely a method of dividing the project into manageable segments in relation to cost and time.

A possible criticism of DSDM is that it is more administrative than the other sub-approaches. It entails comprehensive studies before work is initiated, and constant customer liaison and feedback once it has begun. Also, the documentation concerning the project is administered by what is known as a consortium and is not available for free.

XP (Extreme Programming)

Not to be confused with the Microsoft operating system Windows XP (which is also sometimes referred to simply as XP), Extreme Programming methodology, or XP, is the project of Agile co-establisher Kent Beck (see Chapter 2). On the official site, the discipline is described as follows:

"Extreme Programming is a discipline of software development based on values of simplicity, communication, feedback, courage, and respect."

The following "Core Practices" are outlined:

- Whole Team
- Planning Game, Small Releases, Customer Tests
- Simple Design, Pair Programming, Test-Driven Development,

Design Improvement
* Continuous Integration, Collective Code Ownership, Coding Standard
* Metaphor, Sustainable Pace

(http://www.xprogramming.com)

XP is the most used software development strategy in the United States at the time of this writing. With its extensive and customer-directed planning philosophy, as well as its utilization of "pair programming" (a tactic in which one programmer tests another programmer's work), it has a sound operational and technical basis. The concept of pair programming is expanded by the adoption of the collective code ownership technique, according to which more than one programmer in the team can work on the same code. This technique is further enhanced by the use of uniform code throughout the entire project. Also, it is the customer who establishes quality tests for the development team to implement.

Chapter Recap

* Scrum incorporates Agile's concepts of sprints, user stories, product backlogs, and non-hierarchical team organization into a unique project management system.

* Other project management methods, such as Lean, Crystal, DSDM, and XP, may meaningfully interact with Agile depending on the nature of the project.

| 9 |

Tools for Agile Project Management

In This Chapter
- Assets (Tools) That Facilitate Agile Project Management

A tool in this instance is defined as any physical activity, technique, or software program that accomplishes some purpose within the applied management methodology. If the methodology represents the strategy that governs the project work, the tools are used in the implementation of that strategy. For example, if the project team needs to determine how many productive hours certain iterations will require, there are tools available to assist them in this estimation. Some tools are used to assess the entire scope of the project, from its outset to its delivery of the final product, while others are far more immediate and narrow to provide smaller, more localized solutions.

These tools are either software programs or software incorporated, as opposed to older or more traditional tools such as paper filing systems, Gantt charts and other hard copy planning and assessment systems. Unfortunately, some of the older tools simply do not have the features or capacity to accommodate the techniques used in Agile, since those techniques were not in use when Agile was developed.

Physical Filing/Classification Systems

These systems work to a certain extent in a software environment. It is unlikely that they would appear as an attractive option to many users. Also, they are not easy to transmit to the customer or to remote members of the development team. Software used in assessments or planning typically does not generate physical copies of its output, unless the user dictates otherwise.

Basic Software Applications

These include the traditional style options such as Microsoft Excel or OpenOffice Calculator (or, for Mac users, Numbers). These applications have served their purpose in the past, but modern team management and product development processes have led to the rise of a sub-industry in the development of software that specifically targets the project environment (see the discussion of collaboration tools in Chapter 4). Project participants may find that programs like these are too limited or misdirected in their functionality, requiring extreme improvisation in their use (which does not always make a favorable impression on the customer), or even making some operations in Agile impossible to execute.

Specialized Agile Software

These are the applications that have been designed and marketed specifically for the users of Agile methodologies. Therefore, they are the most suitable for deployment in Agile activities. A number of applications have even been developed by some of the founders of the Agile movement, such as Kent Beck's Extreme Programming.

As with any software, there are open source (freeware) and proprietary programs. The list below mentions some of the most easily available products, but it is by no means exhaustive and is not intended to constitute promotional material.

Starting with the proprietary or trademark software, the following programs are available on the market at this time:

- VersionOne
- Pivotal Tracker
- Rally
- Scrumwise
  (specifically for Scrum teams)

- Agile Agenda
- Agile Bench
- Aldon Agile Manager
- Agile Soup *(Android app)*

- Agile Zen
- Agile Cockpit

The previous list is not a list in any order of priority, and there are more programs available, with more to be released. Some of the listed options offer free trial periods, so interested parties are advised to experiment with different software to determine what works best for their specific project situation before investing.

Turning to open source, which may be used at no charge indefinitely, the following products are available for download. Once again, this is not an exhaustive list, and users should be aware that some open source software does not come with any sort of guarantee.

- Agilefant *(a cloud server that provides a downloadable version of the program)*
- Clearworks
- Express
- FireScrum *(Scrum-specific tool, there are at least ten open source Scrum tools available)*
- Planigle
- XP Studio *(NB: this is NOT Microsoft's operating system)*
- XPlanner+
- Retrospectiva
- Scrinch
- PPTS *(Project Planning & Tracking System)*

Chapter Recap
- Both common office software and specialized Agile software are available to assist with APM.

| 10 |

Practical Implications

This chapter examines the practical issues that arise in situations where Agile is used to manage a project. The issues are categorized under three broad headings: costs, staff, and market implications. These categories seem to be appropriate, given that Agile focuses on and seeks to optimize these aspects of project management.

Expense Structure

Any project usually involves expense of some kind. Whether it is the cultivation of beans in plastic holders for an elementary school exercise or the construction of a bridge over a river, expenditure has to be monitored, and usually predicted, before work begins. Agile serves to reduce or restrict costs in two ways; one of them is very general in its operation, and the other is more an internal function of how the project is managed.

It has already been mentioned that, as opposed to the more traditional and premeditated Waterfall philosophy of "plan first, do next, see if the budget is met," Agile first establishes the budget and then tries to contain the scope of the project within it. This point of departure is the more general of the two ways in which Agile limits the expense associated with a project. The customer or other project commissioner is assured of two things: first, that they won't have to spend more than they are prepared to, and second, that even if their available resources cannot support the ultimate desired outcome, they will at least be left with something constructive to apply in their organization.

This also implies that the customer is never going to be presented with a final result that is not satisfactory to some extent. This eventuality has already been outlined in a preceding chapter. There are some horrific examples of this happening in mega-industry, instances where the development team may have subscribed entirely to the project brief and even overrun the budget and time frame, but delivered a product that was useless to its end user or a failure in its target market.

The second and more microcosmic manner in which Agile cuts costs is through its use of quality monitoring and assessment. This happens on a constant basis, especially in methodologies such as XP or Crystal.

Building a house takes place according to a preapproved blueprint. But it is perhaps more sensible to have the homeowners present to show them the various stages of construction, so that they can refine or tweak the plans as they desire. In fact, people who commission the construction of their own homes usually take a very intense interest in the process and even resort to their own procurement of materials or specialist artisans if they believe that they are able to do the job more cheaply than the primary contractor. This, then, is one of the strengths of Agile.

Staff Issues

The Scrum style of holding meetings may seem immature or showy. However, it does advertise an attitude of urgency to observers, such as customers. Team members are encouraged to adopt the sentiment that the customer's deadline is important and that they need to approach their tasks with a sense of urgency. This is in contrast to premeditated Waterfall projects that sometimes extend beyond their initial deadline and where, in the final analysis, some operatives are exposed as requiring an inordinate amount of time to complete relatively simple activities. This destroys customer satisfaction and distorts perception, since some of those operatives may have been paid according to the time that they spent working on the project.

To refer back to the immigrants' home construction site once more, imagine the laborers arriving at the site in the morning. They first sit around for about an hour or ninety minutes, drinking coffee and chatting about personal affairs. Then they sluggishly start to chop into the hard ground to excavate the foundation, still conversing about their marriages, finances, and sports teams. When the site foreman yells at them to show some enthusiasm, they reply that they still have plenty of time to finish the job. Now compare that scenario with a sprint meeting. It is obvious which approach businesspeople, and society in general, would rather see in action where their money, market share, or other interests are at stake.

Sometimes project or business management systems necessitate the introduction of a supervisory or facilitator role, which is not an inherent part of the organization itself. This role is either partially or entirely dedicated to the implementation of the system. Its job title may even reflect that capacity. As an example, in Scrum there is the ScrumMaster, who does not participate in the concrete project labor but is not entirely a team manager either. There are certain issues related to this phenomenon of dedicated, supplementary roles, whether full- or part-time, that need to be discussed.

First, the person who occupies the role needs to have an above-average understanding of the system. They need to be trained in its application and procedures. Once their role is implemented, they may not be available to perform their usual duties. This may become the focus of envy or antagonism from other staff, since "So-and-so is never at their desk these days," or, as some may ask, "How come they get to go to all the seminars and stuff?"

This type of hostility to implementation needs to be alleviated as soon as possible. Other staff members need to realize that the system is being used for a specific purpose. In introducing the plan to them, the concrete, anticipated ROI or advantages for customer service should be explained in detail, in terms that they can understand. The selection process for the facilitator should also be as transparent as possible, possibly on a voluntary basis. It should be obvious to everyone why a certain person is being used in that role, the extent of his or her new expertise, and why that role is necessary.

Sometimes, employers institute rewards or incentives for staff. This is harder to accomplish when the output of a collective task depends on the contribution of an entire team. Measuring the performance of individual members is not only complicated at times, but also potentially sensitive, especially when the team is engaged in an abnormal or interim endeavor. This is a factor to take into account in selecting and instituting the appropriate Agile methodology.

There is also the usual resistance to new methods, especially where new or atypical techniques are involved. Standing during meetings and using odd terminology are sometimes too hard for the less flexible (or more dedicated) staff members to accommodate themselves to. Once again, the benefits of the system's implementation need to be emphasized at all times.

Another reason the staff need to be properly informed about implementation is that the understanding of its importance empowers them to manage the process themselves, either partially or entirely. The Agile system advocates the use of staff under what is largely their own supervision. The prime example of this sentiment is seen in the Scrum methodology, in which no outside person has authority over how the

Development Team manages and executes the actual project labor. The Team manages itself, mostly, and the ScrumMaster merely provides relevant information and updates on the progress of the project.

When staff take ownership of a situation or project, they are easier to motivate, sometimes requiring no prompting at all. Their level of dedication to the success of the initiative is much higher, and they are likely to be more creative in their input, since they are not blindly following instructions or performing to a bare minimum standard set by someone else. An increased sense of responsibility translates into greater attention to quality and more respect for deadlines, which is harder to achieve in the traditional Waterfall paradigm, where the project manager has greater or even absolute authority and the project scope has already been fixed at its outset.

A possible problem attached to the principle of the exceptionally empowered team is that its internal dynamics may sometimes obstruct its progress. Because of its cross-functional nature, some members may have overlapping or identical skill sets, but subscribe to different approaches within the same discipline. This is obvious territory for dispute and/or paralyzed communication. Another possible objection is that some of the methodologies, XP in particular, might rely on pair programming (see Chapter 4). Not everyone in the software industry supports this technique. However, given the success of XP generally, this seems to be a relatively less significant source of concern.

Market Implications

According to Highsmith (2004), this is one of the focus areas of the Agile movement. Agile's emphasis is on the development and introduction of new products, so the market is better served by a faster turnaround time on such introduction, either in response to its stated needs or as an improvement upon existing options. Enterprises sometimes also have to react in a short space of time to the sudden release strategy of a competitor.

Agile allows for speedy development procedures. Since the process of development and refinement is executed in stages or iterations, the customer can progressively perfect the product or limit its scope, thus enabling a more immediate introduction to the target market. At the same time, they can release an undeveloped version of the product, but market it as a new advance in the industry, then add the remaining stages to later editions.

The constant involvement of the customer in the development process results in greater satisfaction on their part. If they are able to observe the project's progress as it happens, and if they are provided with regular and spontaneous feedback, they may experience the service provided by the developer as superior. Adherence to differentiated time frames is always appreciated, as is staying within the approved budget.

Agile Points of View within an Organization

When implementing Agile within your organization, the system will be perceived differently by various members of the organizational hierarchy. If Agile is implemented properly, then team members throughout the organization stand to benefit.

Executive level managers will appreciate the transparency and efficiency of Agile projects. Using burndown charts (Scrum), product backlogs, roadmaps and other Agile tools, executives can obtain quick high-level insight into project status. Executives also appreciate that Agile is built to be flexible and that each sprint delivers new functionality. If the needs of business change suddenly, then ongoing projects can reflexively change as well. Moreover, since functional products are being developed constantly during the course of a project, there's more opportunity to take products to market quickly and on an ongoing basis. Agile can also facilitate overall higher product quality through the rigorous, ongoing testing mechanisms.

One such testing mechanism is "test-driven development" or TDD, which has been steadily incorporated into Agile Project Management, particularly in the field of software development. TDD is a style of coding whereby programmers create tests that will intentionally fail until a feature has been properly developed. The tests are preserved, cataloged, and continuously implemented throughout production. TDD is used to minimize product defects, which keeps executives happy.

For consumers, Agile's main benefit is, again, its inherent flexibility. Since functionality is released in chunks, products can go to the market in stages and customer feedback can be readily incorporated into the ongoing development of a product. This level of dynamic customization for the benefit of the customer is not offered by the Waterfall method.

Development team members will appreciate the influence and autonomy they gain through Agile Project Management. During Agile projects, it is the team members who prioritize features and determine the goals for their sprints. In Scrum, the Agile team configuration includes a specialized party, the Scrum Master (separate from the project manager), who acts essentially as a team advocate to remove barriers and facilitate communication within the team.

Chapter Recap

- Implementing Agile can require a leap of faith, and you are guaranteed to see some resistance in your organization.

- Benefits of Agile come in the form of lowered costs, more rapid and responsive market engagement, and a more autonomous and empowered workforce.

| 11 |

Brief Agile Case Studies

In This Chapter
• Applying Agile in the Private and the Public Sector

GE

Our first case study, GE (formerly known as General Electric), shows how the system can be deployed in an industry that is not exclusively centered on the development of software, but one that is outside of the pure IT industry. Of course, large corporations usually have an IT department and require development of their own proprietary software, so that is where Agile is most likely to be used.

One example of how GE has used Agile is in its finance department. There, a new software infrastructure was required for crunching numbers so that operatives would be better able to reach informed decisions. Essentially a business analysis intervention, the new software was required to gather data from the existing platforms and make it accessible to the new program. Using traditional methods, the estimated turnaround time for the integration process was between eighteen and twenty-four months.

The integration via the new software, which was executed by GE's own in-house IT department using Agile, took all of one year, inclusive of its implementation.

This type of integration is not uncommon in large companies. Some of them maintain enormous databases of customer information and transaction records. Shifting the entire archive of data to a new, more efficient system, or one which has expanded capabilities, may be a matter either of reducing expenses or of necessity due to a changing market environment. The sooner companies are able to conclude the integration, the sooner they can meet the new expectations of their customers or start saving on costs.

By cutting a year off the development time of the software, GE not only preempted an additional year's use of their prior system, but also eliminated twelve months of developmental expense. This was made possible by the Agile methodology. The more traditional approach, with a fixed project scope and an estimated budget and time frame (such as eighteen to twenty-four months), would have resulted in at least another six months spent in developing the new software.

There also would have been no guarantee as to its absolute suitability. Agile delivers satisfactory pieces one at a time, resulting in an end product that is stable and functional.

Using a more conventional methodology, the summary release of the entire new software package would have necessitated a more sudden and comprehensive integration process, which is not only institutionally traumatic but causes upheaval among staff who have to be taught its use en masse on an immediate, accelerated basis. They also have to waste productive time while the IT personnel work overtime transferring all the data to the new platform and trying to understand errors and how to resolve them. Some of these errors may be systemic and might have been avoided through an incremental approach.

The example cited in this chapter isn't the only area of the enterprise where GE has used Agile. The company has also instituted the methodology in its Industrial Internet range of software products for energy producers, the GE Oil & Gas Engineering Initiative, which has been publicly reported to make use of Agile software development.

Homeland Security

The U.S. Department of Homeland Security ("Homeland Security" or "Department") is an example of a government organization that has implemented Agile in its software development activities. As the federal authority on internal security and border integrity, Homeland Security processes matters such as immigration and the identification of citizens. It has a massive user base (the entire population of the United States), and the standard of its data needs to be impeccable. At the same time, the system used to process and store that data is required to be entirely secure at all times.

The quality of the data and the security of its archiving depend on the sophistication and reliability of the software used by the Department. It is understandable that Homeland Security develops its own software, using its own IT resources, since national databases are highly sensitive and should not be entrusted in their entirety to outside contractors to maintain (even though outsourcing is an existing strategy). In 2013, the Department started to use Agile in its software development (in addition to cloud computing), in an attempt to improve the turnaround time on new projects.

Project Delivery

Homeland Security has an annual budget of approximately $6 billion, with about 15 percent of this budget spent on IT. Agile was implemented in response to an identified weakness in the budgeted delivery of new software products. In 2013, about one in three IT projects exceeded either their budget or their delivery time frame. This concern was addressed by instituting Agile techniques.

The emphasis of the implementation has been on the user. The developers liaise with users, discuss specific instances of user experience, and then allow the users to be involved in the testing of the new software.

In the sense that the end user participates directly in the development process, this is an important method of empowering members of the public in the expenditure of government resources. The internal or citizen affairs department in any country may be seen as slow, excessively bureaucratic, or culpable in the unnecessary absorption of public funds. Through engaging the public in the creation and implementation of new systems and procedures, the electorate may be more amenable to the sentiment that tax revenue is being spent wisely and that the service they receive is the optimum possible experience.

Government Contracts

The competition for government business is a traditional aspect of capitalist economies, and proposals for government projects are sometimes fiercely contested. Homeland Security is no exception to this type of attention from private business. As far as software development companies are concerned, the Department has established an innovative niche use of the Agile methodology in awarding contracts.

Because Agile development takes place in iterations, it is possible to assign each sprint to a different contractor. Remember that each sprint delivers a usable phase of the end product. The entire project can then be spanned over a longer or shorter period of time, postponed, or suspended indefinitely, without the contractor being able to oppose any such decision, or even secure permanent tenure in providing the development service.

This has advantages for government in that an unsatisfactory service provider can be abandoned after their first sprint involvement. Budgetary discipline and the flexible prioritization of new products are also easier to accomplish. These are two of the primary benefits of the Agile methodology, as illustrated by its application in the government sphere.

| 12 |

Extended Agile Case Study No. One

In This Chapter

- A Case Study in Agile

Yahoo! is a multinational firm known for its web portal, Internet search, and related services. With a $32 billion market cap, the company can certainly be called a "large enterprise." What follows is the summary of a case study presented by Yahoo! Agile practitioner Gabrielle Benefield, which describes the process Yahoo! took when implementing Agile. The proof here is not in the pudding, but in the fact that Yahoo! still retains the Agile method of project management despite the challenges they faced during the initial implementation stages.

Implementation

In the environment that is the Internet, the only constant is change. Yahoo!, a company that provides products and services to more than 500 million users worldwide, knew the importance of remaining flexible and adaptive when bringing products to the global, web-based market. Benefield joined the company in 2005 to propel their adoption of Agile Project Management. The goal, starting with Scrum, was to utilize the lightweight framework that Agile methods provide to create "collaborative self-organizing teams" that "effectively deliver products to market." While the following case study outlines many challenges Yahoo! faced, Benefield considers the implementation a success, citing "tremendous successes and valuable lessons learned."

Yahoo! grew tremendously from what was essentially a startup company to a large enterprise. In 2002 they began to pursue a standard process to deliver better products faster. This initiative was based on a program called the Product Development Process (PDP), a Waterfall-type program that had been mandated by Yahoo!'s management. What Benefield found was that many of Yahoo!'s teams and divisions either ignored the process entirely or instead managed to retroactively manufacture participation when they had in fact abandoned the program's methods. Those teams that adhered to the administration's mandated approach found the process more a hindrance than an asset. After debating the top-down mandate of Agile or the bottom-up grassroots method, the enterprise chose to implement the program with the support of the rank-and-file first.

The focuses of dysfunction were the project and team management portions of operations. There were significant shortfalls in the areas of planning, project management, release management, and team interaction. While they were not launched simultaneously, Benefield cites a wish to have launched Agile engineering protocols and project management Scrum methods at the same time. This serves as a cautionary tale; even though the approach was not a top-down initiative, it could have benefited from a wider scope.

Initially, four teams volunteered to test the new Agile methods and share their experiences with the rest of the organization. Their business units were diverse; they ranged from products for customers (email and photo sharing) to internal tools (small business management). Initially the volunteers committed to four directives:

1. To complete comprehensive Scrum training

2. To work with outside Scrum coaches, especially during the period encompassing the first several sprints

3. To use the standardized Scrum protocol outlined by Scrum advocate Ken Schwaber

4. To complete at least one sprint

In keeping with the iterative nature of Scrum and Agile, volunteer teams could opt out of the program anytime after the first sprint. Feedback after two months was positive; managers saw results, and team members liked the system and the experience. This led to a word-of-mouth circulation of the program within the organization, and the praise generated encouraged other teams to express interest in the Agile method.

In lieu of using external coaches, the enterprise shifted to using an internal Scrum coaching team. The purpose of this team was to promote the benefits of the implementation of Scrum within the organization as well as to provide training, coaching, and support for the teams using Scrum. This included ensuring that key events and programs were followed, such as the aforementioned daily stand-up meetings, iteration planning, and sprint retrospectives.

One of the functions of the Agile Project Management system is to identify deficiencies within an organization. As this happened for Yahoo!, who was making the change from a mandated Waterfall system to a grassroots Agile system, Benefield and her team started addressing issues as they arose and making the fixes available for all teams. This meant that in practice, a solution for one team was a solution for all teams. These solutions were Agile-minded, including reductions in bureaucracy as well as improved methods of resource planning and portfolio management.

Tracking Progress

Benefield and her team knew that the only method of measurement would have to be clear and accurate. Across the organization, teams who had implemented the process were solicited for feedback. Those who participated in a survey on the newly-implemented programs received custom-printed T-shirts. This incentive proved effective but may not be a great fit for every organization. It is the responsibility of management to determine how to best incentivize their workforce. In this case, the overall response rate was a surprising 71 percent, fourteen points higher for Scrum pilot team members, and the responses revealed both the huge benefits and the resistances to change. In addition to circulating the promotion of Scrum, these surveys bolstered other teams to get on board with the Agile method.

Support from Management

Feedback from peers was determined to be the biggest factor in management's comfort level with Scrum's adoption progress. The members of the company (the original author of this case study included) who were tasked with expanding the scope of Scrum within the organization tended to brief managers mostly on the benefits rather than the mechanics of Scrum. This approach reinforced the problematic trend of general managers over-focusing on results while under-focusing on methods. Benefield clearly indicates that this led to issues concerning the ability of management to support teams that were dedicated to the adoption of Scrum. It is important to remember that the transition from a mandated Waterfall program to a lightweight adaptive method is a significant change; the fact that Agile methodologies remain relatively newer and more experimental contributes to the resistance that some members of management will inevitably exhibit.

Coaching

Once the framework was in place for the volunteer teams, Benefield's team implemented their engagement model, which allowed them to coach several teams effectively. Benefield states that this model was sensitive to the fact that no two teams would face the same challenges and no two teams would provide the same solutions. This spurred a waiting period for management that was based on the need for Scrum coaches to learn the individual needs of each team they coached. Learning this information allowed coaches to tailor the Scrum architecture to fit the needs of their individual business units.

Coaching also meant not forcing Scrum down employees' throats. Scrum was reserved for those who volunteered to take on the challenges of adopting the new project management program. The initial implementation was organized as follows:

Initial Discussion

- Meet with people within the enterprise who were interested in Scrum, and discuss benefits and challenges.
- Schedule overviews for key members of the team.
- Organize training and coaching, including ScrumMaster training in conjunction with team training.

Preparation & Training

- Work with Product Owner to develop product backlog.
- Conduct two-day Scrum training for the whole team.

Coaching

- For the first sprint, the Agile coach would facilitate the following:
  » First sprint planning meeting

» First sprint review
» First sprint retrospective

For the second sprint, the Agile coach would be present to mentor the ScrumMaster during meetings. During the first stages of this process, the Agile coaches were in frequent contact with the teams to keep their adherence to the process on track. Coaches and facilitators would work with other teams as well to accelerate learning, spot issues early, and pursue improvement. Benefield admits that the first three months were challenging, but the teams that adopted Scrum used it to begin to self-organize and were ready for more advanced training.

Scaling within the Organization

At the end of 2005 Yahoo! had twenty-five teams who were using the Scrum process consistently. Eighty-four percent of team members said the new system was an improvement over the older methods they had been using. However, an internal obstacle arose: a budgetary cycle change forced the entire company to produce more results with fewer resources. This was a challenge for Benefield and her teams, and the company's response is a good example of what to avoid when implementing Agile.

Other teams within the company had heard about how effective Scrum was, either through internal channels or through other professional channels. With little knowledge of implementation or procedure, the individual business units determined that Scrum would be a cure-all for their budgetary woes. Instead of using the professional coaches, many team leaders resolved to learn Scrum on their own, which led to inconsistency and poor interaction between teams. The number of teams implementing Scrum, with and without the support of Agile coaches, rose by a factor of ten. Benefield and her coaches couldn't keep up with the training progress of each team and as a result the entire program was at risk. Teams were denied coaching on the basis of availability but moved forward regardless.

Benefield concluded that while Scrum is simple and appears simple, it can cause quite a bit of change within a team and can change the dynamic between team members. Not everyone is receptive to change, a fact we all know well. The role of coaches and standardized training is to help develop teams through the transition period in which peeling off layers of administrative control can highlight areas of poor performance and dysfunction within a team. Teams often blamed the Scrum methodology as the cause of their challenges when in fact their reluctance to adopt new processes was the root cause. Another issue that arose—and this is very common in organizations that attempt to utilize Agile—is that the team claimed to have adopted Scrum, top to bottom, and to be making excellent progress. A closer look at their methods revealed that what they were calling Agile was in fact a series of mini-Waterfalls. This, too, reflects the unwillingness of many people to discard old habits. These challenges can be overcome with focused training and the use of Agile coaches.

Scaling the Budget

Experience showed again and again that the teams that saw focused and dedicated training also saw the most success. In this period, the coaches still could not adequately train the growing number of teams that were requesting assistance in their adoption of Scrum. Though the implementation program was receiving funding from an internal professional development organization, the demand for training required more coaches than the program could afford. To make her case for additional funding, Benefield implemented a program to gather metrics concerning the effectiveness of the teams that had received adequate coaching compared to those that had not.

The first step in this process was to initiate internal case studies and surveys. The surveys found that there were significant differences in satisfaction and performance between the teams that had coaching and those that had not. Unsurprisingly, the teams with a solid Scrum foundation benefited from the coaching and thrived, while teams that had a poor foundational base or little to no coaching had many ongoing challenges and difficulties. While top-level management was interested in this data, they needed more evidence to release the funds for more coaches.

Once an effective measurement system was devised, Benefield's surveys found millions of dollars in savings and massive increases in productivity ranging from 0 percent to nearly 200. The average productivity increase was about 34 percent. Management was thrilled. Interestingly enough, that number has stayed fairly consistent over time as the program has matured. In 2007 (a year later) the average recorded increase in productivity was 39 percent. From this process Benefield gained some valuable information about the use of Scrum coaches within Yahoo!; remember, this data is specific to Yahoo! and may not be applicable to other implementation scenarios.

- One Agile coach can coach about ten teams per year.
- Each team averages ten people (making the ratio of coaches to staff members 1:100).
- Based on surveyed results, average productivity improvements were about 34 percent.

Refining the Process

Once the money materialized, more coaches could be implemented and the program could be scaled effectively. The expanded coaching program also allowed some mistakes that had surfaced to be corrected along the way. Benefield's team has continued to promote Agile within Yahoo! by creating a culture around it. Promotion efforts include T-shirts and internal communications to recognize the success stories generated by other teams within the company and to promote further adoption or at least openness to Agile. . This is a wise method of adoption: bottom-up instead of top-down.

What We Can Learn

Organizations contemplating the implementation of Agile can learn quite a bit from this case study. It is an exercise in what to do as much as what to avoid. Most important to the entire process is that Yahoo!'s implementation was done from the bottom up with the support and acceptance of the employees, not from the top down as a mandate from the higher level management. The latter scenario is self-defeating in the sense that the creation of an environment in which team members can feel empowered clashes with a managerial assertion of control.

A pitfall, however, was the slow expansion of the coaching team. Organizations need to understand that sweeping changes cannot be effective unless there really is change. Coaches represent a structured and guided path to facilitating that change, and Yahoo!'s ignoring of their role in the process created more work and expense later. This was out of the hands of Benefield's team, but a thorough understanding by all relevant members of the organization would help implement the process.

Gabrielle Benefield's team at Yahoo! worked to adopt Scrum across a large organization by fitting the organization to the program. The following case study summary demonstrates the Intel Corporation's Agile implementation process and how they stretched Scrum to fit their organization's particular needs and protocols.

Chapter Recap

- By anticipating resistance and offering incentives, Yahoo! steadily convinced its employees to buy in to Scrum.

| 13 |

Extended Agile Case Study No. Two

In This Chapter
- A Case Study in Agile

With annual revenues of $38.3 billion and employees numbering 86,300 at the time of this study, Intel Corp. is a world leader in the production of microprocessors, motherboard chipsets, and flash memory products. The case study's focus is on the Oregon and Pacific (OAP) product development engineering (PDE) team and their implementation of Agile Project Management methods. The team needed to implement these new methodologies across multiple teams, sites, cultures, and environments. OAP's work product was a test program designed to run automatic testing equipment (ATE). This is uniquely challenging because no off-the-shelf programming could be used; the program uses a proprietary operating system and interface languages. Prior to the Agile adoption process the team suffered from a number of issues including high turnover rates, poor morale, missed schedules, and insane work weeks. These factors alone present challenges, but additionally challenging to the Agile mindset was the strong Waterfall culture that existed at Intel.

Intel decided to implement Scrum at the beginning of a project, because during the lower-stress initial stages of the project a strong foundation could be developed, and the best practices developed there could be transferred to later stages in the process.

Preparation & Initialization
The first transition group included six teams with numerous sub-

teams. Intel reached out to Danube Technologies Inc. as a Scrum implementation vendor and began the process of transitioning to the Agile mindset. Initially, twenty or so group and technical leads attended focused training in a two-day workshop. Team leaders agreed to commit to a three-month pilot period during which they would use their training "as is" instead of attempting to fit it to the organization. This is an interesting method for promoting adoption, and as the author of the case study, Pat Elwer, notes: "Even though the agreement was there, I could already sense a split in the organization into 'pigs' and 'chickens' in terms of supporting Scrum."[10] Working with Scrum consultants, Elwer determined to advance the following key elements of the ScrumMaster position so as not to create conflict or untoward feelings about the role:

• The ScrumMaster role was valued in performance evaluation as having the same weight as "real engineering work rather than administrative overhead."

• Team members who became ScrumMaster did not have a technical stake in the team's duties.

These stipulations are unique to Intel's circumstance but helped smooth the process by eliminating conflicts of interest and promoting the value of the new Scrum system. At the end of the three-month process, the number of teams to be managed grew from six to seven, with an eighth volunteering to implement Scrum. The challenge then became scaling the program across the organization. Using a scaling model that Danube provided, along with best practices learned in the pilot period and input from teams, the program encompassed twelve

---

[10] For those not familiar with the adage: "In a ham and eggs breakfast, the chicken was involved, the pig was committed."

teams. Again with input from Danube, the teams developed methods for managing and fostering dependencies between multiple teams as well as inter-team communication. What the teams learned from this process can be summarized as follows:

* Adoption is more important than strict adherence.
* Volunteerism is a key to successful adoption.
* Self-organization is a key to and a result of successful adoption.

In the spirit of promoting adoption over adherence, deviations from the "by the book" Scrum methods were discussed but not given negative weight. This method also promoted "outside the box" thinking and accelerated the learning curve for all teams, as well as what Ewer refers to as "unity, not uniformity." Visibility also became a critical component in the implementation process, and channels were developed to allow teams to discuss what worked as well as what proved to be dead-end methods. To fit Scrum into the Intel culture and environment the process was adjusted, and what follows is a brief summary of the roles that key team members played in the process and the program.

fig. 16

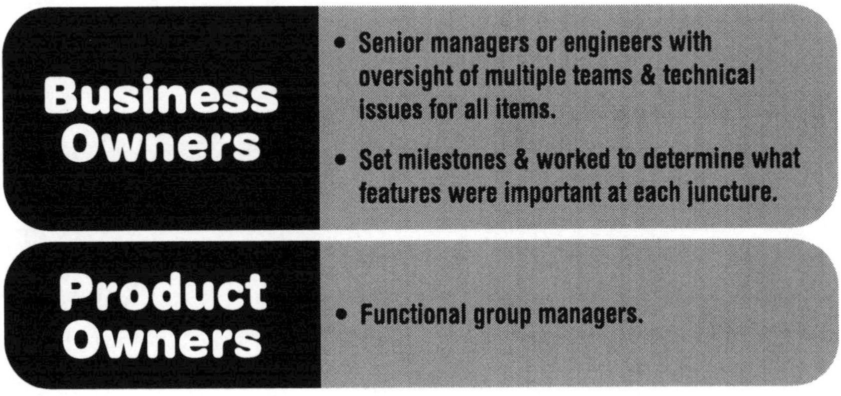

Business Owners
* Senior managers or engineers with oversight of multiple teams & technical issues for all items.
* Set milestones & worked to determine what features were important at each juncture.

Product Owners
* Functional group managers.

127

Technical Owners	• Technical leads who could collaborate to ensure congruence between teams with dependent outputs. • Held meetings to turn epics or novels into sprint-ready stories.
Scrum Masters	• Cross-team engineers with no technical stake in the project team they were Scrum mastering (this prevented a conflict of interest affecting the final product).
Teams	• Team tasked with one particular output of the test suite. • Rarely cross-functional.
Transient	• Team member with highly specialized skills needed by multiple teams. • Moved from team to team as needed by sprints.
Conduit	• Team member who represented more than one person *(i.e. contractors, supervisors, or members of a remote team)*. Could sign up for more story points of work than a normal team member.
Story Owner	• A technical expert with particular knowledge of how to complete a story, who could develop tasks & request participation of certain team members for completion of those tasks.

By the end of the first year, Scrum was fully rooted in the company's decision-making process and was a framework for planning and resource management. Remember, however, that the development was still in the initial "stress-free" stages. The software was only interacting in models. The next step was testing Agile in the execution phase of the process, in which the stakes were higher and the stress on staff and processes was much higher.

The Next Step

Elwer says there were many surprises when the rubber met the road. This period in the production phase is when the silicon devices arrive and information must be gathered about the specific path the project will take toward the future. This is a difficult time in product development engineering. In this period one Scrum team abandoned the new process entirely and reverted to Waterfall techniques for project management. Some other Scrum teams disbanded, deciding that they were finished attempting to use the new system. The remaining teams clung to Scrum vigorously, if not very effectively. Those teams had been using two-week sprints but found them impossible and shifted to one-day sprints instead. There were daily meetings that planned for the next day and reflected on the previous one. In this way they collapsed Scrum's prescribed four meetings into a single meeting under the pressure of the production stage.

These meetings demonstrated the core values of Scrum, according to Elwer. Here could be observed business value prioritization, team sizing, adhering to the backlog, peer updates, implementing process improvements and reviewing the work product. These practices gained pace as the team uncovered more and more information about the devices into which they needed to implement their software. The teams that didn't give up on Scrum remained intact and moved through the process, eventually expanding the sprints back to the two-week standard.

Preparing for Manufacturing

As the testing yielded a more and more bug-free program, manufacturing loomed on the horizon. However, Elwer was still struggling with the effective relay of information within the organization.

Also at this time, in response to existing issues in the software, a number of task forces were being developed. At Intel, a task force is a group of experts who are called to drop everything and address specific issues within development. These groups are effective combatants against crisis-level developmental issues, and their potency was not lost on Elwer. The biggest issue was how to incorporate the task-force approach without changing the overall organizational structure. At this stage, the teams that had retained Scrum through the developmental process were too involved in the work to restructure effectively. The answer was Scrum "feature teams." Adopting the task-force style, this group of technical experts worked like a task force but maintained slots in other teams to give members a cross-functionality as well as a "home" within the project. They served on feature teams "on loan" from their home Scrum teams and represented high levels of collective expertise. The program was a success, not only with the members of the existing teams but also with management.

Elwer makes a list of what went well and what didn't throughout Intel's adoption of Scrum.

What Went Right

1. The unique nature of the "starting from scratch" coding meant that there was little room for error. Tests were often done on live silicon units instead of in software models. This meant that a strong focus was developed on writing good stories and writing good acceptance criteria. Good stories meant good backlogs, and good backlogs meant that the sprints provided their intended results.

   A "pair review" process was developed that called for a developer and a product owner to agree that acceptance criteria had been met.

2. During the determination of velocity for the next sprint, no credit was given for stories that were not completed. This "no partial credit" policy forced teams to focus on 100 percent completion. Stories that did not add up to 100 percent failed for that sprint, and dependent tasks couldn't be started.

3. Use of a nine-day sprint model helped create regularity for the teams. This meant that after sprinting for nine days, review, retrospective, and planning meetings were held every other Friday. Teams would be outside of a sprint every other weekend, and this ultimately improved quality of life and morale. For weekends that fell inside sprints, the teams (using their self-organizing capabilities) could decide whether working through the weekend was necessary to complete tasks on time.

4. Using a structured cadence allowed product owners and business owners to change direction if necessary at relatively frequent intervals.

   Collected data showed a 10 to 20 percent loss of velocity if a sprint was interrupted, so a structured cadence allowed the teams to prevent incurring what they called "sprint interrupt tax."

5. To facilitate the generation of useful metrics like the Burndown Chart, Intel utilized a central, open access tool that smoothed the transition and allowed for continuous and impediment-free planning. Existing programs didn't fit their needs, so they designed their own. Elwer admits that the current offerings are more developed than they were at that time, so the need for an organization to produce their own software is significantly less likely these days.

6. The term "story point" was developed to refer to projects with complex time requirements and tasks that couldn't easily be described as having duration in "days." Using story points made conveying results to upper management and outsiders much easier.

   Reducing tasks to less than a day was liberating for teams and enlightening for management. Tasks were assigned a degree of difficulty measured in story points. If a task took longer than a day, management could identify that the task was probably suffering from an impediment.

7. The Daily Scrum meeting significantly benefited from visuals and graphic representations of progress, with emphasis on the visual Burndown Chart.

8. Use of incremental review, or review processes that didn't wait until the review meeting, allowed developers to change course if necessary before the end of a sprint.

9. Visibility of the backlog and reliable metrics about performance helped managers adjust expectations and revise plans as necessary.

10. Extensive support from upper level management made the transition a success. Elwer claims that an absence of support would have killed the project.

11. To effectively change the behavior of the team members who were adopting the Scrum methodology, the new behaviors would have to be practiced. Consistent use of the program

and sharing of its results has further cemented the Scrum framework into the Intel culture.

What Could Have Gone Better

1. In an effort to improve communication across teams and between product owners and their teams, product owners were allowed to serve on their teams. This worked for some teams, but others found themselves being micromanaged, which is the antithesis of self-organization and presented the company with roadblocks in the areas of communication and lost potential.

2. The maintenance of a large backlog had a negative effect on the teams. They began to feel as though they were being overwhelmed with requests because anyone at any time could edit or add to the backlog.

A solution Elwer's team developed was to segregate new backlog requests from existing ones with a high level of transparency. That way the current backlog was minimal, but "on queue" tasks could still be accessed and assessed for later sprints.

Summary of Results

Elwer measures success in four ways: cycle time, performance to schedule, morale, and transparency. Scrum is identified as the source of a 66 percent reduction in cycle time. In regard to performance to schedule, the two-week planning cycle has been maintained for more than a year since the release of the study. Missed commitments and schedule slips have been virtually eliminated. Morale is trending upward, with improvements in communication and job satisfaction. The transparency provided by the Scrum method has uncovered dysfunctions such as bugs, impediments, weak tools, and poor engineering habits.

What is most striking about this case study is how the Scrum process was stretched to fit the Intel culture and how that culture was elastic enough to accept the change. In both this example and the Yahoo Inc. case study from the previous chapter, the deciding factor in the success of the programs was the dedication of one leader within the organization. That leader's vision and vigilance paved the way for other organizations to consider implementing Agile and assessing the benefits that it may bring.

Chapter Recap

- Intel's adoption of Scrum was met by many challenges, setbacks, and accomplishments.

| 14 |
Criticism

Now that the Agile system has been discussed in some detail, let's explore the criticism it has attracted through the years. Any management theory is susceptible to opposition, either by proponents of rival schools of thought or by those who have identified areas of potential trouble in the approach. Agile is no exception.

Customer Input

One of the primary faults that has been observed in Agile concerns its reliance on the feedback of the end user, or customer. Sometimes, if the commissioner of a project is allowed too great a degree of input or choice in its course and output, the ultimate objective becomes obscured or impossible to achieve on the basis of the preceding work. The aggregation of the work may become so distorted or directionless that it cannot be composed into a satisfactory summary result. This issue may be expressed succinctly in the following adage:

"The customer is always right, assuming that they know what they want."

That the customer is not always sure about their ultimate desired outcome is a reality in the IT industry, as well as in other sectors of commerce where the customer is allowed some level of influence in the decision-making process regarding the nature of the final product. This is seen in the way that some people or organizations can take an inordinate amount of time to choose from the available range of options, or require "consumer guidance" or "specialist advice," even in the selection of such mundane characteristics as color or size. Entire sub-industries of consultants and "experts" have arisen in response to the indecisive nature of financially able yet equally irresolute consumers.

Agile caters to these consumers to a potentially hazardous extent. Giving them the opportunity to provide feedback on a constant basis may cause extra work for the project team or result in conflicting or even directly contradictory instructions regarding the project's scope. Some people, if given the chance to change their minds, will, not so much as a matter of necessity but simply because they appreciate the sense of authority that the exercise endows. Where a substantial amount of their money is involved, they may even feel obliged to enforce that authority, since they are paying to hold it.

The customer needs to understand that the mere fact that they have been asked for input does not necessitate that it be constantly shifting or consistently negative. Some customers are in the habit of being intentionally impossible to please. The way in which the project team accommodates that attitude is more a matter of professional acumen than technical expertise.

As former US President Bill Clinton remarked after the provisionally undecided national election at the end of his second term in office, *"The people of America have spoken, but it's not clear what they said."*

This eventuality is one to which Agile is susceptible. It should be addressed through proper communication with the customer at all times, particularly at the outset of the project, where its risk of arising should be outlined and explicitly discouraged.

Professional Impression/Corporate Image

Effective communication requires time and expense to be sustained. Therefore, any management paradigm that relies on constant communication increases this item of the budget, cutting into the profit margin for the development team and representing a possible source of conflict with the customer. Some customers might not appreciate continuous requests for comment or testing, especially if they are not very skilled in the use of IT or they believe that they pay people to solve such problems for them.

How a business communicates with customers and other outside entities is germane to its public image. At the same time, its inner workings contribute to that image too. Customers need to be presented with a professional, suitably constituted philosophy on business and customer service. Some customers may experience the Agile environment as the opposite of that.

The fact that the Agile team is often temporary in nature may endow it with a sense of having an improvisatory or maverick status. Also, because it is supposed to be relatively more informal than conventional, it may seem too bohemian or artistic to customers who subscribe to a more staid, traditional approach toward supplier relations and product development.

Lastly, Agile does not emphasize the bureaucracy of the project system. Some operators may see this as a source of relief, but it is potentially a disadvantage. They may not even understand how to use the documentation, or they may regard the compilation of their own training material as an undue expense item in the total project budget.

Team Composition

More traditional project management systems require a comprehensive documentation of activity. Together with a larger staff, this ensures that the absence or departure of a team member does not obstruct the future progress of the project. Agile, on the other hand, is somewhat more vulnerable to change insofar as it uses smaller teams and minimal literature or recordkeeping.

Dependency of Interrelated Stages

Sometimes the development of the final product relies on the sequential construction of its component parts, and the later and final phases can only be executed if the preceding ones have already been finished. In project management, this is known as dependency.

Agile has been criticized because it does not provide specific solutions for incorporating *dependencies* into project management. This seems to be a mostly insubstantial point of concern, since the incremental nature of the system results in a steady supply of finite deliverables that interact and comprise the entire finished item. Their interaction is based on their interdependence, so it is apparent that in scheduling the work, the project team would have to incorporate that aspect as an inherent feature of their project roster.

If Agile does not provide a dedicated tool for that aspect, it is perhaps due to the assumption that the project team consists of highly qualified professionals who are not operating on the basis of the linear, unidirectional Waterfall methodology and thus have a thorough understanding of how the project iterations fit together and will automatically realize which elements are dependent on one another. This is possible because the relatively smaller Agile team is responsible for the project in its entirety, as opposed to the more traditional massive project workforces, which are compartmentalized to the extent that some staff may not have any idea of exactly where their output is situated in the overarching scheme of the project.

In Agile, there is also the issue of restrictive iterations. Because the iterations are fixed in their duration and output, sudden adjustments to the scope of the project can necessitate additional sprints. These instantaneous modifications are inherent in the Agile methodology and so, instead of stabilizing the budget and turnaround time, the Agile approach could actually serve to expand them. However, as always, that expansion is only going to be translated into a practical outcome if the customer permits it. If the customer decides to stay with their original budget and duration, they may be obliged to accept a product that is less sophisticated or less developed than what they had hoped for or subsequently realized they needed.

Waterfall

This book has already mentioned the project management strategy known as Waterfall and has provided a rough outline of how it operates, but for the sake of convenience it will now be summarized again. The Waterfall methodology is regarded as traditional or even "conventional" in that it entails a classic plan–execute–observe approach. The problem or market expectation is identified, a response is planned, and then the project work is performed. Afterwards, such as after the release of a new product, the results of the project can be monitored and analyzed.

The typical phases in a Waterfall project are as follows:

- Conception
- Initiation
- Analysis
- Design
- Construction
- Testing
- Implementation
- Maintenance

There is no need to enter into an examination of all the various methods associated with the different phases of this strategy. Obviously, software plays a part in its execution, but the primary sequence of stages remains unchanged. Some may describe it as adhering to a generic rationale or demonstrating a natural progression, in that it maps out how informal, unplanned projects will run their course anyway.

What has also been noted about the Waterfall methodology is that it generates a rigid project scope, but only an estimated budget and time frame. Therefore, it is prone to cost more or take longer than anticipated. It also does not necessarily deliver a product that is entirely or even remotely adequate for the desired outcome.

Considerations such as these are typically raised when Waterfall is compared to Agile. This juxtaposition is an unsurprising exercise in the management advisory industry (see Chapter 11), but it is not merely due to professional rivalry or intellectual one-upmanship. The advantages of Agile over Waterfall have been established in practical applications, not limited to the IT industry. The two case studies in this text serve as proof of that.

What may limit the extent of the evidence at this time is the relatively short history of the Agile methodology. It was only officially inaugurated as a project management philosophy at the start of the twenty-first century, and the literature and operating track record of the system are not as prolific as those of the older approaches. Therefore, it is possible for objections to Agile to arise because it is a "new" system of management. Where valuable resources of time and capital are at stake, some economic role players prefer to stay away from what they see as unproven or precariously novel attitudes. They may also refer to their traditional organizational culture in making this assertion.

However, after more than ten years in service and a publicly reported resume of success in both big business and government, this objection is starting to seem increasingly false and inflexible. As more enterprises adopt the Agile methodology in one form or another, those who remain steadfast in Waterfall or other approaches may start to lose market share or industry stature. Those who do *not* remain adherent to traditional methods may experience progress in the opposite direction, either through increased customer numbers and retention or by association with other esteemed companies that use Agile. What follows is a short summary in table form of the main differences between Agile and Waterfall. It is probably one of the most published diagrams in project management literature at this time, but no publication on the subject of Agile would be complete without it.

fig. 17

WATERFALL	AGILE
Fixed Scope	Variable Scope
Single Execution Phase	Iterations (Sprints)
Summary Delivery	Incremental Delivery
Estimated Budget & Time Frame	Established Budget & Turnaround Time
Inflexible Blueprint	Constant Adjustment of Scope Possible
Limited Opportunity For Feedback	Iterative Feedback Required
Top-Down Management	Self-Managed Teams
Less Transparent Management	More Transparent Management
Segregation of Skills	Cross-Functional Teams
Extensive Administration	Minimal Bureaucracy
End User Examines Finished Item	End User Tests & Makes Increments
Terminates Only On Completion	Possible End-Point After Each Iteration

The system that is used depends on the nature of the project and the required staff. There is no purpose in trying to ascertain the superiority of one system over the other. Project managers simply have to try to match a system to their specific project characteristics.

Chapter Recap

- Due to the mercurial quality of customer demand in IT, Agile's reliance on customer feedback can prove inconsequential.

- Agile's breakdown of customary hierarchies may come into conflict with an organization's professional aesthetic.

- Agile's iterative methodology may prove incompatible with projects that require specific sequences of production.

| 15 |

The Agile Sub-Industry

In This Chapter

- Agile Consultants, Trainers, Certifications, and Literature

As is the case with other management systems, such as business or organizational management methodologies, Agile has attracted a sub-industry of experts, practitioners and product suppliers. These professionals rely on their advanced knowledge of the Agile system and its methods to provide advisory and implementation services to their customers. Some of these firms also design and publish Agile tools, such as the software described in Chapter 10.

The Sub-Industry

Some experts offer Agile techniques as part of their entire portfolio of management options. Others are dedicated exclusively to Agile. This sole focus is seen among those who established the paradigm, such as Kent Beck, the founding authority on XP (Extreme Programming), who has a website committed to XP and Agile.

The extent to which this sub-industry has achieved success or is proliferating is a matter of future observation. In relative terms, Agile is a very new management discipline and, although it has been adopted by thousands of firms, its true value will only become apparent after a matter of decades.

There are two possible impediments to its progress. The first is that Agile is not a broad enough discipline to merit official academic status. It cannot stand on its own as a subject. It is merely one of a variety of project management approaches and does not independently possess the magnitude or complexity of subject matter to constitute a separate field of study.

At the same time, because it is so lacking in complexity and minimal in its philosophy and methods, it can be assimilated into an organization's processes without outside assistance. Management can easily examine and apply its procedures. The fact that the software tools are openly available on the market, sometimes at no charge, enables the frequency of this occurrence. Contrast this to business management systems such as Six Sigma, which requires advanced statistical expertise to master, or the Toyota Production System (Toyotism), which affects the entire organization top to bottom.

The absence of more official academic recognition deprives a subject of supporting infrastructure. Its promotion and development then relies on the contributions of its loyal proponents, which are more sporadic and undeveloped than the regulated, officially sanctioned and sponsored study and improvement enjoyed by more traditional disciplines.

There are, however, organizations with authority in the industry, the foremost of these being the Agile Alliance, a nonprofit organization that offers registered membership and aims at an international subscription. The Alliance undertakes academic research projects and endorses workshops and conferences.

Another option, which is focused specifically on Scrum, is SCRUMstudy (http://www.scrumstudy.com). SCRUMstudy administers certification programs for those who wish to practice as Scrum experts, either as employees in an enterprise or as management advisers. Trainees are required to pay fees and pass examinations. These courses can be undertaken through the international network of partners with whom SCRUMstudy is associated.

Literature

Literature on Agile might not be as substantial or easy to obtain as that of other management systems. The new nature of the paradigm translates into a shortage of published subject matter. Most of the literature, therefore, is comprised of articles and papers. However, a few books are available for those who desire to conduct further reading, and we recommend starting with an important work by one of the seventeen founders, Jim Highsmith, heading the list below:

Agile Project Management: Creating Innovative Products (2nd edition) by Jim Highsmith (2009).

Coaching Agile Teams: A Companion for ScrumMasters, Agile Coaches, and Project Managers in Transition by Lyssa Adkins (2010).

Agile Testing: A Practical Guide for Testers and Agile Teams by Lisa Crispin and Janet Gregory (2009).

The Enterprise and Scrum by Ken Schwaber (2007).

Scrum Shortcuts without Cutting Corners: Agile Tactics, Tools and Tips by Ilan Goldstein (2013).

Schwaber (author of *The Enterprise and Scrum*, above) is another of the seventeen Agile founders. Besides these works, readers are advised to peruse the peripheral material available online.

Chapter Recap

- An abundance of Agile resources exist across a multitude of mediums.

conclusion

The software industry is a modern phenomenon and, as such, the techniques of management and product development that it entails are somewhat unique to its character and product. To say that Agile could *only* have originated from this industry is not entirely accurate, but it is a partially cogent statement. Perhaps Agile merely required the environment presented by the IT sector to be more formally adopted.

As a member of the more general catalog of project and business management techniques, Agile has a worthy position and offers an effective approach to the management of suitable projects. Its efficacy has been proven by its diverse, extensive application in practice and its stature in discussions of management systems.

The extent to which it progresses into the future, in terms of both expansion and refinement, remains to be seen. However, the simplicity and universal relevance of its principles and innate philosophy would appear to suggest that it will be present in management textbooks for some time. Agile may start to acquire an even greater presence as more and more industrial activity relies on IT and the development of custom software.

One should also remember that some principles in management are timeless. Just as those twentieth century immigrants slowly but patiently constructed their homes piece by piece in their new country, so too does Agile represent some of the overriding concepts in business, management, and the design and release of new products in any industry. Perhaps, rather than just a trendy catchphrase or a temporary phase, Agile is representative of the culmination of a long-term evolution, supported now by technology that more fully enables its effective implementation. As far as its success is concerned, only time will tell.

glossary

Agile Project Management Framework
Also referred to as the Agile Project Management Life Cycle. This term refers to a five-step, iterative product development process: Envision, Speculate, Explore, Adapt, and Close. Contrast with "Waterfall."

Dependencies
A general project management term used to describe tasks that must be resolved in a specific sequence—task A must be done before task B.

Feature
A particular service or functionality that a system provides and that is valued by a client.

Online Collaboration Tools
Nickname for the variety of applications that are Internet-accessible and can be used to facilitate work and collaboration between multiple team members. Online collaboration tools are often used to boost productivity in virtual environments.

Product Backlog
Used in Scrum to list and organize desired features of a product.

Product Data Sheet
A concise and metrics-focused document that offers a summary of project targets and progress.

Product Owner
A role typically seen in Scrum, the product owner is usually the project's chief visionary and principal stakeholder.

Product Roadmap
A tool used to assess and visualize requirements, timetables, and task priority levels for a project.

Project Charter
A general document that defines the purpose and success standards of a project.

Project Management
The process of coordinating and regulating a collective approach to the execution of a task.

Project Manager
Oversees the day-to-day operations of a project, addresses questions of priority, scope, and responsibilities.

Project Sponsor
Obtains funding and other resources for a project and ensures that the development team and project stakeholders are on the same page.

Scrum
A spin-off of Agile Project Management that incorporates sprints, product backlogs, retrospective meetings, and several other Agile utilities and principles.

Sprints
The essential development units in
Agile Project Management, typically
one week to one month in duration
and focusing on the development of a
certain set of features.

Sprint Velocity
The average number of story points
resolved during a sprint.

Sprint Structure
The process of planning sprints by
estimating workloads associated with
various features and distributing similar
workloads between sprints.

Story Points
A metric used to quantify the
complexity of user stories.

User Story
A short, one- or two-sentence
structured testimonial that provides a
customer's perspective on the need for a
product.

Waterfall
Sometimes referred to as the "Waterfall
method" or the "Waterfall approach."
A traditional project management
methodology that emphasizes a
plan and definition of success that
is substantially more rigid than that
of the Agile approach. The five steps
of Waterfall project management
are Initiating, Planning, Executing,
Controlling, and Closing.

about clydebank

We are a multi-media publishing company that provides reliable, high-quality and easily accessible information to a global customer base. Developed out of the need for beginner-friendly content that is accessible across multiple formats, we deliver reliable, up-to-date, high-quality information through our multiple product offerings.

Through our strategic partnerships with some of the world's largest retailers, we are able to simplify the learning process for customers around the world, providing them with an authoritative source of information for the subjects that matter to them. Our end-user focused philosophy puts the satisfaction of our customers at the forefront of our mission. We are committed to creating multi-media products that allow our customers to learn what they want, when they want and how they want.

ClydeBank Business is a division of the multimedia-publishing firm ClydeBank Media LLC. ClydeBank Media's goal is to provide affordable, accessible information to a global market through different forms of media such as eBooks, paperback books and audio books. Company divisions are based on subject matter, each consisting of a dedicated team of researchers, writers, editors and designers.

For more information, please visit us at :
www.clydebankmedia.com
or contact _info@clydebankmedia.com_

Your world, simplified.

notes

WANT FREE AUDIOBOOKS?

connecting authors & readers

HOW DOES IT WORK?

sign up **select book**

get email **read & review**

1. Sign up by visiting www.revizea.com/signup and select what types of books you are interested in receiving.

2. You'll receive weekly e-mails from Revizea listing the latest titles available to you for free.

3. Select a title and format (print, ebook, or audiobook) by completing the corresponding online form.

4. Await confirmation that your request has been approved (approximately 24 hours.)

5. Receive your title, read (or listen), and leave a review.

39606207R00093

Made in the USA
Middletown, DE
20 January 2017